T0293164

Ransomware Analysis

This book presents the development of a classification scheme to organize and represent ransomware threat knowledge through the implementation of an innovative methodology centered around the semantic annotation of domain-specific source documentation. By combining principles from computer science, document management, and semantic data processing, the research establishes an innovative framework to organize ransomware data extracted from specialized source texts in a systematic classification system.

Through detailed chapters, the book explores the process of applying semantic annotation to a specialized corpus comprising CVE prose descriptions linked to known ransomware threats. This approach not only organizes but also deeply analyzes these descriptions, uncovering patterns and vulnerabilities within ransomware operations. The book presents a pioneering methodology that integrates CVE descriptions with ATT&CK frameworks, significantly refining the granularity of threat intelligence.

The insights gained from a pattern-based analysis of vulnerability-related documentation are structured into a hierarchical model within an ontology framework, enhancing the capability for predictive operations. This model prepares cybersecurity professionals to anticipate and mitigate risks associated with new vulnerabilities as they are cataloged in the CVE list, by identifying recurrent characteristics tied to specific ransomware and related vulnerabilities.

With real-world examples, this book empowers its readers to implement these methodologies in their environments, leading to improved prediction and prevention strategies in the face of growing ransomware challenges.

Ransomware Analysis
Knowledge Extraction and Classification for Advanced Cyber Threat Intelligence

Claudia Lanza, Abdelkader Lahmadi, and
Jérôme François

CRC Press
Taylor & Francis Group
Boca Raton London New York

CRC Press is an imprint of the
Taylor & Francis Group, an **informa** business

Designed cover image: © Shutterstock

First edition published 2025
by CRC Press
2385 NW Executive Center Drive, Suite 320, Boca Raton FL 33431

and by CRC Press
4 Park Square, Milton Park, Abingdon, Oxon, OX14 4RN

CRC Press is an imprint of Taylor & Francis Group, LLC

ISBN: 978-1-032-83210-4 (hbk)
ISBN: 978-1-032-86750-2 (pbk)
ISBN: 978-1-003-52899-9 (ebk)

DOI: 10.1201/9781003528999

Typeset in CMR10 Font
by KnowledgeWorks Global Ltd.

Contents

Foreword

[1] Nowadays we can say that the specter of ransomware is haunting the World. The different types of these dangerous malware, capable of holding your data hostage until a ransom is paid, have become a growing threat to individuals, businesses, and even big infrastructures. In recent years, the annual number of ransomware attempts worldwide has been around four hundred thousand. For this reason, is crucial studying cyber threats to identify and classify the basic mechanisms of ransomware models. In the face of this sophisticate and continuously evolving challenge, one crucial step towards effective defense lies in understanding the ransomware variants and their unique features. This book investigates ransomware from a semantic perspective, thus it is a precious resource for anyone seeking to navigate the ever-evolving landscape of ransomware classification. Along the chapters, the authors expertly analyze and classify cyber threat models and build a ransomware corpus, digging into the various aspects employed by cybersecurity experts and professionals. Analyzing the knowledge contained within documentation related to cyber threats, this book opens the path to cross-disciplinary studies in the area of cyber attacks. It explores the different perspectives from which carry out research work on the categorization of ransomware knowledge bases. The twofold approach combines principles from computer science with those from document management and representation as a means to organize ransomware datasets from specialized source texts in an ontology structure. Whether you are a cybersecurity analyst, a social engineering researcher, or someone looking to augment the knowledge in these very significant fields, this book offers a comprehensive exploration of the key factors that define cyber threats and ransomware variants. You will look at the diverse attack vectors exploited by ransomware, from exploiting vulnerabilities in software to attacking human vulnerabilities through cyber-attack campaigns. The authors accurately analyze the different vulnerability classification models, the attack patterns, and the existing cybersecurity knowledge graphs. Moreover, they show how to build a ransomware knowledge base, enabling readers to distinguish between more rudimentary and sophisticated variants. Furthermore, the book explores how to build a ransomware corpus and discusses semantic modeling and knowledge classification. The classification of ransomware extends beyond technical details. This book, in fact, combines the analysis of cybersecurity mechanisms with knowledge management principles and practices. This comprehensive approach empowers readers in not just identifying and classifying ransomware threats, but also addressing the main aspects of their potential impact for implementing cyber threat intelligence strategies. By equipping the readers with a deeper understanding of the ransomware world, this book empowers them to become more vigilant experts in the fight against cybercrime. As the authors meticulously map the maze of ransomware variants, the reader gains the knowledge necessary to navigate this complex landscape and develop intelligent ways to safeguard precious information and critical digital resources.

Professor Domenico Talia, Universitá della Calabria.

---

[1]The quotations of Serrai, Bianchini, De Francesco et al., Guerrini, Marradi, Cesanelli, Biagetti, Gaio, Pazienza, Gnoli, Folino, Lavazza, Mazzocchi, Marino, Rosati, have been included by translating them from Italian to English.

Preface

In the ever-evolving landscape of Cybersecurity, the threat posed by ransomware continues to escalate, both in sophistication and in its impact on businesses and individuals globally. Traditional defense mechanisms often lag behind, leaving significant gaps in our ability to predict and mitigate these threats. This book seeks to bridge this gap by introducing a novel approach to understanding and combating ransomware through a throughout analysis of exploited vulnerabilities, and the application of semantic annotation to classify these threats more effectively.

The core of this book revolves around a groundbreaking methodology that employs semantic annotation of Common Vulnerabilities and Exposures (CVE) descriptions, a practice that has traditionally been underutilized in the domain of cybersecurity. By annotating CVE related to ransomware, this book develops a detailed knowledge base that categorizes ransomware exploited CVE and their associated tactics, techniques, and procedures. The semantically annotated CVE descriptions provide data on (i) the shared common causes that can lead to ransomware; (ii) the most usually attacked platforms given certain causes; (iii) the general likelihood through which the ransomware is able to be performed;(iv) the most typical condition according to which the ransomware begins, being it remotely or locally executed ;(v) the most common impact a ransomware provokes according to the aforementioned values; (vi) the most common action an attacker will undertake when performing a certain ransomware under given conditions and impacts; (vii) the most common effect a given ransomware has given all the aforementioned factors. The purpose of the semantic annotation process is to create a combined matrix of information, a structured knowledge base, able to represent the typical behavior of certain ransomware starting from the vulnerabilities' descriptions. The human-based semantic annotation results represent the basis from which to automatically predict the likelihood a ransomware shows while presenting similar characteristics, leveraging the knowledge gained from the pattern-based approach over the vulnerability features learned through the text annotation process. This enables a deeper understanding of how specific vulnerabilities are exploited and provides a structured framework that can be leveraged for enhanced predictive threat intelligence.

The methodology presented here is not merely theoretical but is a product of rigorous interdisciplinary research. It combines principles from computer science, document management, and semantic data processing to build a classification system that not only organizes ransomware data effectively but also makes it operationally actionable. By integrating this classified data within an ontology framework, the book facilitates a comprehensive view of ransomware attacks. This structured knowledge enables cybersecurity professionals to anticipate potential ransomware attacks by recognizing the recurring features associated with specific vulnerabilities.

Furthermore, the book explores how the integration of ATT&CK (Adversarial Tactics, Techniques, and Common Knowledge) frameworks enhances the classification scheme, providing a more granular understanding of ransomware operations. The goal is to automatically discover the correspondences on a three-level dimension: Ransomware-CVE-Tactics&Techniques. This three-way classification represents the basis to further improve the ontology system to represent the information around ransomware in a taxonomic scheme where the hierarchical disposition of concepts results in a configuration of classes and sub-classes. This approach not only contributes to the academic field by proposing new techniques for the realization of classification tools but also empowers practitioners with methodologies to analyze the behavior of ransomware in relation to exploited vulnerabilities.

As you journey through the pages of this book, you will gain insights into the intricate processes of data annotation, the challenges of semantic classification in a cybersecurity context, and the practical applications of this research in real-world scenarios. Whether you are a cybersecurity professional seeking to enhance your strategic capabilities, a researcher interested in the latest methodologies, or a policy maker looking to understand the implications of ransomware, this book aims to serve as a valuable resource.

By the end of this book, readers will be equipped with the knowledge and tools to not only understand the "how" and "why" behind ransomware attacks but also to foresee and forestall future threats. Welcome to a new era of cybersecurity, where advanced knowledge extraction and classification pave the way for more proactive and resilient cyber defenses.

Authors

Claudia Lanza is currently a Research Fellow at the University of Calabria. After a yearly visting abroad period as PhD student with the TALN group at the University of Nantes, she obtained a PhD title in 2021 in ICT on a thesis focusing on the Semantic control within the Cybersecurity domain. In 2023 she was Visiting Researcher in Nancy at LORIA working on the creation of cyber-attacks classification tools as a means of guaranteeing a monitoring semantic activity in Cybersecurity triaging procedures. Her research interests cover Information Science, Documentation, Information Retrieval, Knowledge organization and representation, and Specialized domain-oriented terminology systematization.

In this monograph Claudia Lanza is the author specifically of the whole Chapter 1; for Chapter 2 is the author of Section 2.1; for Chapter 3 is the author of Section 3.2. and Sub-section 3.2.1; for Chapter 4 is the author of Section 4.1. and Sub-sections 4.1.1., 4.1.2, 4.1.2.1, 4.1.2.2, Section 4.2. and Sub-sections 4.2.1, 4.2.2, and Sub-section 4.3.2.

Abdelkader Lahmadi is an associate professor in computer science at University of Lorraine, teaching at ENSEM engineering school and doing research at LORIA and Inria in RESIST research team. Abdelkader's research interests are in the area of cybersecurity and threat analysis in networked systems (IoT, industrial systems, 5G, etc.). More in detail, he is investigating innovative solutions in the area of automated cyber security using AI for anomaly detection, mitigation, and proactive approaches. In this area, he developed and patented a technology, named SCUBA, for discovering in an automated way the attack paths that can be exploited by an attacker through the assets of a given network. He has a Ph.D. and engineering degree in computer science. Since 2018, he has been the head of ISN (Digital Systems Engineers) degree at the ENSEM engineering school in Nancy. He has been the scientific director of the LHS (High Security Laboratory) in Nancy since 2020, specializing in experimentation and analysis for cybersecurity research. Throughout his professional career, Abdelkader has contributed to numerous software developments and prototypes to validate his scientific research. He is a co-founder of CYBI, a spin-off of University of Lorraine and Inria focused on automated cybersecurity solutions using AI systems for attack path management.

Jérôme François is a senior research scientist at the university of Luxembourg in the research group SEDAN (Service and Data Management) at SnT (https://wwwen.uni.lu/snt/research/sedan) and is an affiliate member of LORIA and INRIA Lab in Nancy, France where he was a researcher and deputy team leader of RESIST team from 2014 to 2023. He received a Ph.D. degree in computer science from the University of Lorraine, France, in December 2009. His area of research is network and service management but with a focus on security management. He developed a strong scientific expertise and practical experience in the adaptation and application of Machine Learning methods in this area. This covers different topics such as anomaly detection, phishing prevention, botnet modeling, or honeypot and darknet monitoring as endorsed by his publications. He participated in different national and European projects (SPARTA European Cybersecurity Competence Network,

French PEPR on cybersecurity, H2020 AI@EDGE, H2020 SecureIoT) and was leading the NATO international research project ThreatPredict. He developed strong partnerships with industries (e.g. Orange, Thales) and academia (joint teams with University of Waterloo in Canada and Osaka in Japan). He is a core member of network and service management community by taking several responsibilities regarding conference organization and by leading IRTF Network Management Research Group (NMRG). He is the co-founder of Cybi (https://www.cybi.fr/), a cybersecurity startup built on top of research results regarding attack path management.

In this monograph Abdelkader Lahmadi and Jérôme François are the authors specifically of the whole Chapter 2 except for just Section 2.1; for Chapter 3 are the authors of Section 3.1, and Sub-sections 3.1.1, 3.1.2, 3.1.3, 3.1.4, 3.1.5, Section 3.3, and Sub-sections 3.3.1, 3.3.2 ; for Chapter 4 are the authors of Sub-section 4.1.2.3, Section 4.3 and Sub-section 4.3.1.

The three authors jointly collaborated for the Preface and Conclusion sections.

List of Figures

List of Tables

1

Classification and Knowledge Representation

In this chapter the classification procedures will be described by first examining some of the main considerations from the literature on the conceptualization framework of reality. This will include an exploration of *extensional* and *intensional* approaches, as well as the various types of classification commonly found in fields such as bibliographic studies, including enumerative and faceted approaches. The last part of this chapter will be dedicated to the classification domain knowledge organization and representation systems, by delving into the overview towards the description of the taxonomies and the ontologies, being the latter the classification tool chosen for the purposes of this research activity on ransomware knowledge systematization. The structures already existing within the Cybersecurity field of study from a semantic perspective are most of the time designed in a taxonomic direction usually expanded in an ontological configuration, as it can be observed in the analysis provided in Chapter 2. To be compliant with the granularity of information shared by the communities of experts, this research study presents the construction of a classification tool following the hierarchical structure characterizing the taxonomies extended through an ontology framework able to better represent the semantic connections among the domain-dependent concepts.

1.1 What does It Mean to Classify

Classification refers to the organized grouping of a series of real-world objects. This task stems from the need of both creating a conceptual framework of the reality and of providing a systematization of the information produced by mankind. Serrai (1977) [116] in his manuscript on the classification seen from a philosophical and information science perspective precisely highlights the proliferation of written documents in an extensive time span, and this has contributed to the necessity of defining retrieval procedures to identify the ones to be consulted. The author specifically refers to the different variety of documents persons encountered over the years, going from clay tablets to historical, legal, religious, literary, administrative, and cultural documents, to those housed in archival structures for public access. Hence, given the heterogeneity of documents persons can access, it is crucial to find them in a correct and efficient manner included in a *niche* which should "be in an intrinsic connection with their semantic content and in a perceivable relation with a group of niches" (1977:24).

Documents can be considered objects of reality in classification activities since they are placed at the edge of the elements making up the conceptual framework to be organized. In the literature much focus has been placed on the association of the classification procedures to the partitioning tasks over the reality characterized by the existence of several

DOI: 10.1201/9781003528999-1

symbols, which need to be organized for the sake of providing a certain order and systematization. The principle of subdivision of the entities composing the world is specifically described by Serrai in his work. Indeed, the author states that the process of classification is the "assimilation of objects considered sufficiently akin to take a common identification" (1977:8). The competences acquired during a specific time frame over reality's elements, according to the author, are segments that can provide better results in terms of knowledge classification. Indeed, the processes related to the organization of the entities within the reality are strictly connected with the perspectives of "constituting a number of classes, or concepts, that reduce the high variety of reality into a more handling group of reference elements". Therefore, to start the classification procedures, one should fix the existence of "categories of differentiation of objects which will overlap to the classes' denomination; the identification of objects according to one (or more) of these categories; the ordering of the categories based on a principle, intrinsic to the classes and objects semantics, or external to that" (1977:9). This work results to be significantly precise in the way the classification is described as the activity of dividing the reality into classes, which are necessary to explain the complexity of the world they are included in.

According to De Gros (1899), there are some principles to follow when classifying the objects belonging to the reality system:

1. Classification according to the generality order or likeness: this kind of classification gathers the objects in classes whether they present a certain type of characteristics in common;

2. Classification according to hierarchies: this type of classification implies the grouping activity over the objects according to levels;

3. Classification according to the genealogy: the objects are grouped following derivation or kinship rules;

4. Classification according to teleonomic structures: this type of classification manages the reality and its elements under the lens of their usability and aim.

Definition of the classification criteria is a very complex activity since it assumes the capability of modelling how the explicit knowledge expressed within the documents is associated to the implicit knowledge constituted by the categories of interest.

Erika de Francesco et al. (2009)
A methodology for semi-automatic classification schema building

---

De Francesco (2009) [47], alongside several similar studies in the literature, defines two commonly adopted approaches in the construction of classification schemes: *extensional* and *intensional*. The *extensional* approach involves gathering the documents in "sub-systems, according to adequate *similarity* measures computed according to a cluster of features", while the *intensional* approach refers to the definition of classes tasks as "aggregation, reduction, specialization and generalization". As Guerrini (2013) [60] stated, the classification procedure means to "group together objects or concepts showing common features, distinguishing them from the objects and concepts not owning those characteristics. The common elements in a class constitute the characteristics or division principles". (2013:371)

In order to identify the conceptual boundaries within which a different group of concepts are meant to be detected, a *fundamentum divisionis* should be fixed, and this is the principle according to which the *extensional* classification gathers the objects belonging to one or more groups since they share given features. De Francesco (2009) describes in detail the steps pursued in applying the *extensional* approach, including the arrangement of the features alongside the creation of an *attributes' matrix* where "the objects onto which perform the classification" and the "properties whose status are going to be taken into account to maximize the inner homogeneity and the mutual heterogeneity among classes (i.e., the variables or the column-vectors of the matrix)" are clearly depicted. In her work the author mentions the difficulty that can come up in the selection of a correct number of features given the association between a substantial group of features and a good classification that should detect all the sides of a certain phenomenon of reality.

Through the *intensional* approach, the "concept related to a class is being created and clarified through the definition of its semantic edges with the concepts related to other classes" (Marradi 1992 [85]). Among the attributes that constitute the system by which an *intensional* classification detects the persistent properties of an object to which a position has to be given, Marradi cites semantic fixity and the use of it as a means through which the research of the main characteristics should be owned by those objects. Marradi also provides a detailed description of the operations usually accomplished in the classification tasks. In particular, he also expands on the differences between the two approaches by stating that whereas for the *extensional* approach in classification a set of events are grouped in several sub-systems as to "maximize the similarity among the members of the same sub-system and the dissimilarity among the members of different sub-systems", the *intentional* approach relates to the process of "conceptual explication or clarification". Regarding this latter approach, the author continues by giving the following details: "By assigning a different term or expression to each concept related to the several classes, the bi-univocal relations of concept-term are enhanced given the implicitly oppositive nature of each semantic assignation". In this way the concept of the *fundamentum divisionis* is covered by Marradi, the framework of the concepts is partitioned to build the "concepts of classes".

According to Serrai "Classes are constituted by those objects owning the features envisaged by the categories and the criteria they specify and determine the classes themselves. The elements included in the classes express their *extension* or denotation; the properties that characterize those elements or justify their membership to the classes express their *intention* or understanding or connotation" (1977: 19). The *intensional* approach, following the considerations of Serrai, is the most suited to the semantic classifications.

When a set of features characterizes a certain group of concepts, a class is formed. The process of classification actually requires three elements: a) the "existence of categories for differentiating objects which will match the classes' denomination"; b) "the identification of the objects according to one (or more) of those categories"; and c) "ordering the categories on the basis of a principle, intrinsic to the semantics of classes or objects, or external to this semantics" (Serrai 1977). Given that objects can easily be connected to many semantic structures, the definition of given features, acting as edges, results to be fundamental in the subdivision process characterizing the classification schemes' systematization. Indeed, Serrai's insights are explicitly precise in the identification of the main logic behind the classification procedure, i.e., the need of establishing a certain *property* capable of "differentiating the species" given the number of times it is applied in order to achieve "dichotomous subdivisions": classes containing these properties and others lacking them. [1]

---

[1] Classification systems are broadly employed within the librarianship field of study as methods to group together a series of objects belonging to a specific discipline by detecting common attributes. In this sense, the literature is significantly marked by the works carried out by prominent figures as Birger Hjørland, Lois Mai Chan, Geoffrey Browker, Diego Maltese, Carlo Bianchini, Claudio Gnoli, Alberto Petrucciani, Michele Santoro. In this book specific attention has been paid to the description of the underlying logic of the classification approaches to identify the main operations undertaken in the subdivision of reality objects.

1.2   Hierarchical-enumerative and Faceted Classification

Within the framework of Library Science the need of employing a given structure to classify the knowledge has represented an essential issue to address. The methods implemented in this context are essentially based on two approaches: the hierarchical-enumerative classification and the faceted classification. The former is considered to be a monodimensional system and the latter a more expanded way to establish the relations among the concepts proper to a given knowledge domain.

More specifically, the principle of enumerative-hierarchical classification schemes addresses the formalization of the categories under which the elements belonging to a specific knowledge sphere are placed. Cesanelli (2008 [31] considers these traditional classification systems where each element "owns a correct and univocal place within a unique scheme, wide and hierarchically deep, and it can be found through father-son categories path". As the author states, this system is a monodimensional type of classification since it encompasses just one principle of classification to differentiate the classes. In this case, as Serrai highlights, the classification can be named *dendritic* since it implies a system of bifurcation once a branch of elements strictly connected to a certain element is created, not necessarily showing semantic areas in common. For instance, the author uses the Dewey Decimal Classification (DDC) as a representative case of dendritic subdivision of elements representing the universal knowledge. This type of bibliographic classification was developed in 1873 by the librarian Melvil Dewey, where the criterion of subdivision is associated with the conceptual framework distribution in ten main classes, the decimal numbering system that allows the "monodimensional ordering with infinite hospitality" (Serrai, 1977). The DDC is a classification linked to a documentation framework dealing with a certain kind of knowledge and is based on ten main classes, referred as disciplines, which in turn are subdivided by a descending decimal numbering in divisions and sections. The structure beyond the DDC is meant to be connected with the three mental notions forged by the philosopher Francis Bacon to read the knowledge within the reality of the world: memory, reason, and imagination (Wiegand, A. 1998 [131]). Thanks to this reference tripartion, the DDC classifies the knowledge around ten main classes, i.e., disciplines, further subdivided into more specific ones in a tree-form structure following the decimal numbering. Each time a specification of one element is needed, the DDC system provides a subordinated class until the information required is reached. Enumerative classifications are based on the settlement of predetermined categories, meaning that a set of predefined categories representing a distinct topic or concept that keep being static in the classification scheme. These top-level categories are established in advance and remain fixed. The number of categories is predominantly limited and this jeopardizes the compliance with the evolution of knowledge specific to given domains.

Another typology of classification, based on the DDC and widely used in Library Science, is the analytic-synthetic system, the facted systematization of knowledge, which derives from a representative figure within the domain – Indian librarian Shiyali Ramamrita Ranganathan - who developed the Colon Classification in 1933. Although inspired by the work of DDC on the organization of knowledge, Ranganathan identified some limitations, such as the reduction of themes discussed in a work when building an overview of the subjects as well as an update of other ones [24], and he "formulated the principles of a new one approach that would have allowed them to be overcome through a system based on decomposition and recomposition operations of the subjects to be classified" (Folino 2013:423 [46]).

Following Gnoli's words (2004:10) [55], the Colon Classification: "mainly consists in the decomposition (analysis) of the concepts composed in their own simple parts, the so called isolate. Each isolate can be expressed through annotation that is obtained by a proper table. The pieces of this annotation are reassembled (synthesis) according to an established quotation order. Therefore, this method has been also called analytic-synthetic". This allows for a highly articulated terminological branching/taxonomy, an element that provides a detailed level of association from a semantic point of view between terms that represent concepts of some domain. The fundamental principle formulated by Ranganathan was the subdivision of the main theme of documents in five categories: Personality, Matter, Energy, Space, Time (PMEST) [45]. "The facets are, therefore, the multiple expressions of the reality, the ways of being identified by the categories" (Lavazza 2002) [76]. In detail, retracing the considerations of Bianchini (2006) [23], the Personality has a more philosophical assumption since it represents the objects of study belonging to the variety of disciplines section; Matter refers to the properties or materials, and Energy are actions and processes occurring in a given discipline [107]. The other two categories are linked to information about the spatial and temporal dimensions. With respect to this segmented scheme which has guided the analysis of the documents existing in a librarian context by decomposing the features in a more entangled network of aspects, in the 50s the Classification Research Group (CRG) developed a more expanded way to represent the different faceted systematization to classify the objects of reality by integrating to the PMEST a group of other fundamental categories: object, type, part, properties, material, process, operation, agent, patient, sub-product, space, and time (Mazzocchi e Gnoli 2006 [87]).

Compared to the hierarchical approach, where the information is investigated in a monodimensional way by assessing the kinship to one discipline, the faceted methodology allows more expanded analysis of the subjects related to the documents. In this regard, Marino (2004) [84] states that "These systems, avowedly alternative to traditional hierarchical-enumerative schemes, are in fact the result of a radical rethinking of classification techniques: by abandoning the idea of a priori enumeration of all classes in favor of a methodology that allows for the creation of categories 'on the fly' starting from some previously decided elements (the facets and foci), the classifier is also finally assured, when indexing the material, of the possibility of generating the classes he needs". As Rosati (2003)[2] points out, the main advantages of using a horizontal approach, such as faceted classification, are *multidimensionality*, since each element of the reality in the faceted system is classified through a wide range of facets; *persistence*, where the objects of a certain spectrum of knowledge gets represented by intrinsic attributes, or facets, as highlighted by the author, allowing a solid classification systematization almost independent from external changes; *scalability*, being the core feature of the faceted systems since this characteristic allows the exponential increase of a set of objects to classify in order to create a new form of description of a new property; *flexibility*, in this sense the author refers to the possibility to carry out a research on the basis of one or more facets, creating the path for another core element of the faceted analysis, i.e., *composition*.

Being more flexible, faceted classifications enable domain-oriented information to be organized in a more dynamic way dividing each concept into a variety of facets, which represent the different features of those concepts. The principle of composition, proper to this type of classification, provides users with a multi-dimensional acquisition of information based on specific subject research within a field of study.

While faceted classification offers numerous valuable benefits by considering the combined procedure to analyze documents from an inverse disaggregation perspective, in this specific work the enumerative-hierarchical approach was employed to classify the information about ransomware, retrieved from highly specialized types of documentations. This decision

---

[2]https://www.itconsult.it/contrib/uploads/La-classificazione-a-faccette-fra-Knowledge-Management-e-Information-Architecture-parte-I.pdf

was made since a vertical scalability of attributes constituting classes results to be more compliant with the existing tools on cyber attacks classification.

> In the literature a wide range of bibliographic classification systems have been created during the several historical periods, among which, following the detailed list provided by Guerrini (2013) [60], Expansive Classification (EC), by Charles Ammi Cutter (1837-1903); Dewey Decimal Classification (DDC), by Melvil Dewey (First publication: 1876); Classification Decimale Universelle (CDU) (1905), forged under the basis of the DDC and developed by Paul Otlet e Henri La Fontaine, specifically with the purpose of universally comprehend all the areas of study which they conceive as interdependent subjects and particularly dealing with the scientific documentation; Library of Congress Classification (LCC); Bibliographic Classification (BC) by Henry Evelyn Bliss (1935); Colon Classification (CC) by S.R. Ranganathan (First edition: 1933).

1.3   Semantic Annotation for Classification Purposes

The literature on the classification schemes development shows a variety of approaches, among which those concerning the semantic annotation of source corpora have demonstrated that an in-depth labeling of textual data can lead to a subdivision of concepts meant to represent the main classes in a semantic framework. As stated by Liao et al. (2011) [79] a semantic annotation model can "help to bridge the different knowledge representations. It can be used to discover matching between models elements, which helps information system integration" (2011:61). The authors specifically refer to the meaning of semantically annotate a text and precisely provide a connection to the classification procedure once this approach is used to "enrich target object's information" (2011:63) of a specific field of study. Kim et al. (2006) [71] present a work based on the construction of a taxonomy classification method starting by the annotation of meaningful parts of texts in input. The authors precisely indicate that, in order to obtain a classification system, "A small number of *meaningful* sentences are essential to understand the contents of texts and these contribute to improved taxonomy classification" (2006: 1174). The authors associate to texts a set of *Cue phrases* supporting the identification of semantics meant to be analyzed and normalized to create the hierarchical structure. In this sense, the article addresses the importance of the concepts selection phase which would represent the starting point from which to extract meaningful portions of sentences to be considered as patterns towards classes development. As argued by the authors "some sentences are more essential in order to understand the contents than others, and terms from *important* sentences should be identified in the classification process". In the context of Cybersecurity, the use of semantic annotation, identified as a task to discover salient information in given texts, is quite extensively shared by a range of studies. For instance, Phandi et al. (2018) [105] employed NLP to extract information from the Cybersecurity reports, a method specifically named "SecureNLP" and it is aimed at discovering the main features of malware. The authors specify that the annotation is performed through the use of the Brat Rapid Annotation Tool (Stenetorp et al. 2012 [122]) which "marks the words and phrases that describe malware behaviors and map them to the relevant attribute labels, which are the labels we extracted from the MAEC vocabulary. There are a total of 444 attribute labels, consisting of 211 ActionName labels, 20 Capability labels, 65 StrategicObjectives labels and 148 TacticalObjectives labels" (2018:698). Abdullah et al. (2019) [6] also consider the semantic annotation a useful way to identify meaningful information in textual segmentation referring to cyber attack knowledge systematization. The authors present a state of the art of the existing semantic annotation tools and describe the annotation of the corpus for the cybersecurity documents. Bridges et al. (2013) [27] also address the issue of labeling cybersecurity-related documentation and specifically oriented their study to the annotation of textual segmentations belonging to CVE using the Common Weakness Enumeration (CWE) taxonomy to map the labels. The authors carried out a study in line with the proposed research activity in this monograph, although they strictly focused on the annotation of the vulnerabilities while in this research the focus is on the association with the ransomware exploiting them. The automatic labeling described by the authors is based on the detection of the relevant terms within these descriptions according to a prior list of terms which enabled a symmetrical matching procedure. The labels used by the authors are the following: "software vendor", "software product", "software version", "software language", "vulnerability name" (these are CVE-IDs), "software symbol" (these are files, functions or methods, or parameters), and "vulnerability relevant term" (2012:4). The work proposed by Bridges et al. (2013) underlines a relevant aspect when treating specialized domain-oriented documentation. In detail, the authors point out that in the literature related to cybersecurity strategies there is a lack of "specific training data", since the labels developed to describe the entities belonging to the very specific fields of study are not extensively shared in the scientific communities. Conversely, the tools usually trained to identify salient segments of textual data are not targeted to specialized concepts retrieval, they tend to be more general by using for example systems such as OpenCalais[3], Standford Named Entity Recognizer[4], or the NERD framework (Rizzo and Troncy 2012 [111]). The study of Joshi et al. (2013) [69] is cited as one of the main attempts of providing a labeling structure for the Cybersecurity domain always starting by the analysis of CVE descriptions, as well as that of McNeil et al. (2013) [88] who created an algorithm to be implemented in order to extract the information covering the vulnerabilities and the exploits data. Joshi et al. (2013) specifically investigate the way the unstructured typologies of databases within which the information about Cybersecurity is contained can be structured from a semantic perspective to allow an easier management of specialized knowledge. To achieve this goal, the authors propose the implementation of RDF-linked data representation for the concepts related to this field of study starting from the National Vulnerability Database (NVD) e using ontologies and DBpedia knowledge base. As Bridge et al. (2013), also this study shows the limitation in using existing annotation tools to label the specialized textual information, given their more generic nature to broadly cover many domains in terms of entities such as common places, people, or organizations. The research activity presented in this monograph results are highly similar to the system theorized by Joshi et al. (2013) especially in the concepts identification phase. Indeed, the authors established a group of the following seven classes, which are the ones meaningful to represent a vulnerability:

- Software: It represents the target software and operating systems (e.g. Microsoft .NET Framework 3.5, Ubuntu 10.4)

- Network Terms: It represents information related to networks (e.g. SSL, IP Address, HTTP)

- Attack: It is subdivided in Means and Consequences that represent respectively the way to attack (e.g. Buffer overflow) and final result of an attack (e.g. Denial of Service).

- File Name: (e.g. index.php)

---

[3]https://www.w3.org/2001/sw/wiki/Open_Calais
[4]https://nlp.stanford.edu/software/CRF-NER.shtml

- Hardware: It represents the target hardware (e.g. IBM Mainframe B152)

- NER Modifier: This always follows Software or OS and helps in identifying software version information.

- Other technical Terms: Technical terms that cannot be classified in any of the above mentioned classes.

As in the proposed research activity in this monograph addressing the ransomware knowledge systematization starting from CVE description, the investigation of Joshi et al. (2013) have defined both a selection of each class in order "to represent key aspects in the identification and characterization of an attack" (2013:4), and the development of RDF representation starting from the information extracted by these texts. Dealing with textual information within specialized documentation to perform semantic annotation procedures, Pech et al. (2017) [104] argue that the annotation of texts is usually executed over unstructured documents and the isolation of the main representative concepts appears to be strictly connected with the contexts in which they occur. For the authors the process of semantically annotate texts is "functional to obtain better results in the semantic search because the documents are represented in a conceptual space" (2017:2). Successively they provide a set of tools to perform this approach, among which DBpedia Spotlight, Gate, or Ontea, which is useful to run a pattern-based task over the documents under analysis, and when citing Castells et al. (2007) the authors address the issue of using ontologies for the "annotation classification", a principle followed in their work. The use of an ontology to annotate a group of documents making up the source information from which to start formalizing a specialized domain is a common task documented in various works, such as Cabada (2018) [53], Kiryakov (2003) [72], Yuan-jie (2012) [134], Xu (2019) [132], More (2012), [91] Markis (2020) [82] to cite a few. In this research the ontology will represent the final step in the classification scheme development for the ransomware knowledge systematization. Indeed, the first phases are based on the analysis of the source documentation to detect a recursive structure of sentences which can lead to meaningful concepts, as Kim et al. (2006) highlighted. Secondarily, the concepts identified as representative are interpreted as main classes to which associate a series of trigger expressions aimed at identifying the sub-classes in the taxonomic structure.

1.4 Classification-oriented Domain Knowledge Organization and Representation Systems

As mentioned previously, classification involves organizing the conceptual framework of reality in a structured manner. Stock (2010) [123] considers concepts as "the smallest semantic units in knowledge organization systems". According to Hjørland (2009) [62], concepts are "building blocks" of certain knowledge frameworks. The way concepts are organized to be part of the classification schema is managed via conceptual systems that facilitate the representation of the taxonomic levels of knowledge domains.

A Knowledge organization system (KOS) is made up of concepts and semantic relations that represent a knowledge domain terminologically. In knowledge representation, we distinguish five approaches to KOSs: nomenclatures, classification systems, thesauri, ontologies and, or a borderline case of knowledge organization systems, folksonomies. Knowledge domains are thematic areas that can be delimited, such as a scientific discipline, an economic sector, or company's language. A knowledge organization system's goal in information practice is to support the retrieval process.

Wolfgang G. Stock. 2010
Concepts and Semantic Relations in Information Science

In order to guarantee a more systematic organization of concepts belonging to specific domains of study, the construction of semantic tools, supporting classification scheme development, allows one to get oriented in the vast spectrum of technical knowledge. These tools facilitate access to specialized knowledge frameworks and are known as Knowledge Organization Systems (KOSs). As Hjorland (2016) [63] points out "The two main aspects of KO are (1) knowledge organization processes (KOP) and (2) knowledge organization systems (KOS). Knowledge organization processes (KOP) are, for example, the processes of cataloging, subject analysis, indexing, tagging and classification by humans or computers. Knowledge organization systems (KOS) are the selection of concepts with an indication of selected semantic relations. Examples are classification systems, lists of subject headings, thesauri, ontologies and other systems of metadata". KOSs are semantic structures employed when it comes to supporting the retrieval of sector-oriented information and structuring data in a conceptualization framework to help users to be oriented within specialized fields of study and informative systems to interpret the information to share. Zeng (2008) [135] highlights several aspects related to the KOS' functions in knowledge management and as structured data discovery means by bringing together several key figures in the semantic studies such as Hodge (2000) and Koch (2004).

[...]These systems model the underlying semantic structure of a domain and provide semantics, navigation, and translation through labels, definitions, typing, relationships, and properties for concepts (Hill et al. 2002, Koch and Tudhope 2004). Embodied as (Web) services, they facilitate resource discovery and retrieval by acting as semantic road maps, thereby making possible a common orientation for indexers and future users, either human or machine (Koch and Tudhope 2003, 2004).

Marcia Lei Zeng. 2008
Knowledge Organization Systems (KOS)

In fact, KOSs are employed for knowledge organization and information retrieval, and "they promote knowledge management; iii) they are knowledge representation structures based on terminology" (Souza 2012:183 [112]). The following picture, taken from the work carried out by Souza et al. and taken by the studies of Hodge and Koch, represents the different types of KOS (Figure 1.1). In the realm of Cybersecurity background, a plethora of KOSs continues to grow with the aim of managing a continuously evolving terminology asset to support the information retrieval operations. For instance, MITRE is a constantly updated platform where one can find a variety of information related to the cyber-attacks executed on the infrastructures (CAPEC), the Vulnerabilities (CVE), and Weakeness (CWE) exploitable by the cyber threats and the Platforms being attacked (CPE). Through these

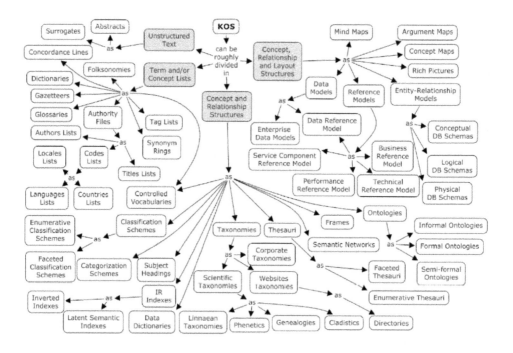

FIGURE 1.1
KOS types as defined by Souza et al. [112].

portals, thoroughly described in Chapter 2, it is not only possible to retrieve authoritative information to be used as reliable source corpora from which the information to be processed is extracted, but also to understand the enumeration and classification process characterizing the field of the cyber-sphere which has undergone a validation step by experts of the domain. For instance, CAPEC is organized in two main categories: by domains of attacks and by mechanisms of attacks, which in turn are subdivided into several other subcategories carrying on certain attributes hierarchically representing the techniques employed to attack a system. Other official sources of specialized knowledge published by authoritative institutions, which are marked by a reliable level of specificity in the way the spread the domain-oriented data, are for example the NIST 7298r2 – Glossary of key information terms, the ISO 27000:2016 – Information technology – Security techniques – Information security management systems – Overview and vocabulary, the Sophos Threatsaurus – The A-Z of computer and data security threats, the NICCS – National Initiative for Cybersecurity Careers and Studies – A Glossary of Common Cybersecurity Terminology. In the works carried out on cybersecurity-related ontologies: Obrst L., Chase P. More specifically targeted to malware formalization works, Rastogi et al. (2020) [108] developed a malware ontology for threat intelligence tasks, namely *MALOnt*, Ding et al. (2019) [40] expanded the subject of malware individuals and family through the use of the ontology conceptual systematization, Mundie et al. (2013), [92], and most recently Keshavarzi et al. (2023) [70] focus on the use of ontologies to represent the information around digital extortion attacks. Among other studies carried out in the Cybersecurity domain referring to ontology structures development it is worth mentioning the contributions of Obrst (2012); [96]; Oltramari et al. (2014); [98] Parmelee (2010); [101]; Souza (2022) [48]; Singhal and Wijesekera (2010); [120]; Aviad, Wecel, and Abramowicz (2015); [15]; Takahashi and Kadobayashi (2015); [126]; Doynikova et al. (2019) [42].

1.4.1 Taxonomies

Amongst the systems used to organize and represent the specialized knowledge, a taxonomy is defined as "a controlled vocabulary consisting of preferred terms, all of which are connected in a hierarchy or polyhierarchy". (ANSI/NISO Z39-19:2005₉). The construction of the hierarchy follows the principle of enumerative classification systems, which relies on vertical subdivision based on specific characteristics to assign elements to a main class. "When several fundamenta are considered in succession through a series of intensional classifications, a taxonomy is produced. Specific concepts/terms (such as taxon, rank, clade) are needed to deal with taxonomies"(Marradi 1992:129 [85]). De Francescco (2009) [47], in this regard, states that the "taxonomies consider the hierarchical structure management: this implies that all the specializations of the same type must be on the same level of generality". Even though this approach, following the author's observation, could lead to many types of specialization in accordance with the "achievement of the exaustivity", the strategy of detecting a certain *fundamentum divisionis* entails the grouping of these elements in highly specialized levels. In the processes of organization of given knowledge domains, taxonomies serve as a means of organizing concepts in a nested categorization approach to establish semantic relationships within knowledge domains. The hierarchical arrangement of concepts in taxonomies reflects the level of granularity within the represented areas of study, with a model of incremental specificity. Despite their tree-like structure, taxonomies can be scalable systems that enrich classes with specific specifications as needed. Each category is subsumed within a higher-level parent category, maintaining inclusiveness while ensuring clarity and precision in classification. This hierarchical relationship signifies inclusiveness, as subcategories inherit the attributes and characteristics of their parent categories. However, each category remains distinct and mutually exclusive within its hierarchical context, ensuring clarity and precision in classification. The hierarchical systematization of concepts also facilitates the information retrieval by deepening the information from a broader level of data integration to the more specific degrees guaranteeing a better precision in the knowledge acquisition and improving the efficiency and effectiveness of organizing and accessing vast amounts of information. Indeed, in a taxonomy, such as the Linneo's binomial taxonomy, per each level there is a set of referred concepts organized into nested categories, allowing to access to information from a diverse perspective. Di Nunzio (2014) [39] affirms that "A taxonomic structure created for a specific scientific domain [...] 'translates' the natural language with the corresponding conventional language, allowing the semantic categories learning targeted to the reference domain, as well as possible similar application in other fields of knowledge". As far as the type of hierarchical connections fixed for the concepts is concerned, Stock (2010) [123] points out that "In a taxonomy, the IS-A relation can be strengthened into ISA- KIND-OF (Cruse, 2002, p. 12). A taxonomy does not just divide a larger class into smaller classes, as is the case for simple hyponymy. A taxonomy fulfills certain conditions, according to Cruse (2002, p. 13): Taxonomy exists to articulate a domain in the most effective way. This requires "good" categories, which are (a) internally cohesive, (b) externally distinctive, and (c) maximally "informative".

1.4.2 Ontologies

Ontologies are one of the types of KOSs functional for the purposes of providing a conceptualization of reality. Indeed, the main definitions provided by the literature refer to this specific feature of conceptualizing the contexts of determined fields of study. Gruber (1995) [56], for instance, states that "An ontology is an explicit specification of conceptualization". For Schreiber, Wielinga and Jansweijer (1995) [58]"An ontology is an explicit, partial specification of a conceptualization that is expressible as a meta-level viewpoint on a set of possible domain theories for the purpose of modular design, redesign and reuse of knowledge-intensive system components". Borst (1997) [26] added to the definition provided by Gruber the adjectives *formal* and *shared*, stating that the ontology is a "formal specification of a shared conceptualization", reaching, by quoting Guarino et al. (2009) [59], the following definition offered in 1998 by Studer [125], "An ontology is a formal, explicit specification of a shared conceptualization". For Uschold (1996) [128] "An (explicit) ontology may take a variety of forms, but necessarily it will include a vocabulary of terms and some specification of their meaning (i.e. definitions)". The author also specifies that ontologies can be distinguished according to their degree of formality. Therefore, there are the "highly informal: expressed loosely in natural language; semi-informal: expressed in a restricted and structured form of natural language, greatly increasing clarity by reducing ambiguity; semi-formal: expressed in an artificial formally defined language; rigorously formal: meticulously defined terms with formal semantics, theorems and proofs of such properties as soundness and completeness". Uschold and King (1995) [129] provided a precise set of definitions to the key phases characterizing the ontology development: (a) the ontology capture: "identification of the key concepts and relationships in the domain of interest, i.e., scoping"; "the production of precise unambiguous text definitions for such concepts and relationships; the identification of terms to refer to such concepts and relationships; the agreeing on all of the above"; (b) the ontology coding "explicit representation of the conceptualisation captured in the above stage in some formal language. This will involve committing to some metaontology choosing a representation language and creating the code"; "Integrating Existing Ontologies"; "Evaluation" and "Documentation".

A deeper specificity implies a less generic type of ontology, as outlined in Biagetti (2010). The author precisely distinguishes among the different forms of representing knowledge domain concepts in an ontology systematization. In detail, Biagetti (2010:7) makes a distinction among several types of ontologies:

- *top level ontologies*, the ones that support the representation of general concepts, the so-called "universals of knowledge" which are not dependent on the domains;

- the *domain ontologies*, these kinds of ontologies support the schematizing of specialized knowledge in compliance both with the corresponding domain and with a wide range of principles proper to specific areas of study on which communities of experts share their vision and provide a detailed spectrum of exhaustive descriptions;

- the *task ontologies*, in this case the ontologies allow the formalization of concepts that refer to a given activity;

- the *application ontologies* which deal with the formalization of a specific activity within a scientific dimension.

In the presentation of the ontologies, as "means created with the purpose of defining in a formal way the nature and the structure of whichever organized system, of making explicit the entities - concepts, objects, processes - and the relationships between them, of making clear the hierarchical relationships correlating the concepts and making all of this understandable in a machine-readable language" (Biagetti 2010:13) the author directly addresses the issue of creating a biunivocal connection between objects and concepts. For Biagetti "Different types of ontologies represent the reality based on different levels of conceptual abstraction, they use a language characterized by a different level of formalism and expressivity" (2010:15). The common specification highlighted by the majority of authors regarding ontologies resides in their capability of representing a specific domain by grouping the key concepts into a system of classes and sub-classes. In particular, according to Chandrasekaran et al. (1999:22) [32] "Ontologies generally appear as a taxonomic tree of conceptualizations, from very general and domain dependent at the top levels to increasingly domain-specific further down in the hierarchy". Medina Nieto (2003:4) [95] points out, in this regard, that, assuming that ontologies are the semantic means by which knowledge proper to specialized fields of study can be represented and managed by informative systems through the use of structured machine-readable grammar, "The terms and relations are clearly defined in that domain; There is a mechanism to organize the terms, (commonly a hierarchical structure is used, as well as IS−A or HAS−A relationships); There is an agreement between users of an ontology in such a way the meaning of the terms is used consistently". This is a remark also underlined by Gilliam et al. (2005) [54] for the pivotal role they envisage in the terminology since it helps in defining and constructing ontologies. The authors clearly stress the importance of choosing the terminology that has to be coherent in order to guarantee an effective way of communicate in the scientific community. The hierarchical structure by which concepts are represented by domain-oriented terminology represents a key point through which the ontologies are strictly connected with the taxonomies and the intensional approach in classifying the objects of given domains. "The backbone of an ontology consists of generalization/specialization hierarchy of concepts, i.e., a taxonomy" (Guarino, Oberle, and Staab 2009:2).

In computer science, ontology is, in general, a 'representation of a shared conceptualisation' of a specific domain. It provides a shared and common vocabulary, including important concepts, properties and their definitions, and constraints, sometimes referred to as background assumptions regarding the intended meaning of the vocabulary, used in a domain that can be communicated between people and heterogeneous, distributed application systems.

Jeff Z. Pan. 2009
Resource Description Framework. Handbook on Ontologies (pp71-90)

The conceptualization of a specific knowledge domain in ontologies is possible thanks to the employment of specific languages that follow the principles of Description Logics (DL). Baader (2009) [17] broadly describes the process of using these knowledge representation language models, stating firstly that the reason why DL is taken as reference model to describe the knowledge domain under investigation is to be found in its process of describing concepts as "expressions that are built from atomic concepts (unary predicates) and atomic roles (binary predicates) using the concept and role constructors provided by the particular DL" (2009:23). In particular, following the considerations of the author, DL "provide their users with various inference capabilities that deduce implicit knowledge from the explicitly represented knowledge. The subsumption algorithm determines subconcept–superconcept relationships". Therefore, the way the concepts are expressed in a DL framework follows the criterion of assigning them specific definitions and relationships. One of the syntaxes usually employed in the representation of concepts within an ontology systematization is the Resource Description Formalization (RDF) language. RDF is built upon a logic of triples in the form of *subject – predicate – object* (W3C Recommendation). "To represent RDF statements in a machine-processable way, RDF defines a specific extensible markup language (XML) syntax, referred to as RDF/XML. RDF-annotated resources (i.e. subjects) are usually named by Uniform Resource Identifier references. Uniform resource identifiers (URIs) are strings that identify Web resources. Uniform resource locators (URLs) are a particular type of URIs, i.e. those having network locations" (Pan 2009: 73). In RDF "predefined Web resources rdfs:Class, rdfs:Resource and rdf:Property can be used to define classes (concepts), resources and properties (roles), respectively.[...] RDFS does not predefine information properties but a set of meta-properties that can be used to represent background assumptions in ontologies" (Pan 2009). For Biagetti (2010) [22] formal language such as the Web Ontology Language (OWL) shows a stronger expressivity in specifying ontologies, explaining that it is a language "thought to be used in applications that can treat the content of information, the meaning of terms and the relationships among terms. It widens the RDF Schema, uses the same syntax as RDF and its basics grammar, but allows to have a greater number of relationships among the classes: cardinality, equality, disjunction, and adds the capability of expressing more information related to the features of the properties, such as the symmetry" (2013:19). The formal language of OWL can be expressed in an ontology in three sub-languages, as Antoniou and Van Harmelen (2003) [11] clearly identify.

Formal language of OWL

1. OWL Full: The entire language is called OWL Full, and uses all the OWL languages primitives. It also allows to combine these primitives in arbitrary ways with RDF and RDF. Schema. This includes the possibility (also present in RDF) to change the meaning of the pre-defined (RDF or OWL) primitives, by applying the language primitives to each other.

2. OWL-DL: OWL DL (short for: Description Logic) is a sublanguage of OWL Full which restricts the way in which the constructors from OWL and RDF can be used.

3. OWL-LITE: OWL Lite excludes enumerated classes, disjointness statements and arbitrary cardinality (among others).

The choice between OWL DL and OWL Full mainly depends on the extent to which users require the meta-modeling facilities of RDF Schema (e.g. defining classes of classes, or attaching properties to classes).

Antoniou and Van Harmelen, 2003
Web ontology language: OWL

The authors also provide readers with a checklist of advantages and disadvantages in choosing one of these three languages. In detail, for what concerns OWL FULL the positive side is related to the compliance with RDF, while, on the other side, it seems to be quite complex to interpret. OWL DL is a type of OWL language that "permits efficient reasoning support", it is uncomplicated both from a user and machine perspective. Ultimately, OWL Lite appears to have a "restricted expressivity". Biagetti (2010) further provides a set of parameters to characterize the main sub-languages in OWL, stating that the first type, OWL FULL, though it is considered as the one completely compliant with RDF syntax, is not able to offer a semantic and logic representation as OWL DL does. Indeed, the latter, "allows the maximum of the expressivity ensuring the complete computation and decision-making process". According to Pazienza (2010:36) [103], an ontology is able to express the "connections among concepts/objects/events and stands as a description of the worlds through:

- Concepts (in hierarchically organized classes)

- Properties and attributes (of each concept)

- Constraints (on the properties and attributes of a concept)

- Instances (which may not exist for some concept, or for all of them)".

The author emphasizes the importance of ontologies in creating a representation of a reality, formalized as the *domain*, by creating a set of classes of objects with the main aim of "providing a partial specification of a set of conceptualizations for a computational system [...]"(2010:37). According to Pazienza, developing an ontology should start with the "axiomatization of concepts' definitions and of the related relationships". This implies a solid knowledge of the terms representing the *domain* under study, as they are the starting point to refer to a specific concept that can create the preconditions to the classes' construction. Indeed, following the considerations of Pazienza, the concepts are essentially the "objects (names) and relations (verbs) of the world of interest". Once the specific terminology of the domain is acquired, the concepts are set in a hierarchical structure, using the main relation of *subClassOf*, which entails the inheritance process typical of the ontology systematization processes. This relation means that "each time A is a subclass of B, every property valid for the instances of B can be applied to the instances of A too" (Pazienza 2010: 48). As noted by Gaio et al. (2010:107) [52], ontologies have two main functions: "1) to determine what is there, what exists or may exist, i.e., which entities are the ones constituting the reality; 2) to determine which are the characteristics of the entities and their relations". In this work an ontology using the sub-language OWL DL will be presented, it will include the concepts related to ransomware behavior by collecting them in a set of classes. These classes will consist of several sub-classes, which are linked to the principle of *extensional* representation of a class in the classification procedure. Moreover, the classes will be characterized by several features and relationships with other instances, referring in this case to the *inclusion* approach described in the section dedicated to the classification approaches. The main purpose of the formalization of ransomware knowledge in an ontology structure is to build a KO tool to classify the information about this technical field of study guaranteeing an explicit and complete representation of the knowledge specifically referred to cyber attacks in a taxonomic perspective.

2

Cyber Threat Knowledge

In this chapter a set of existing systems explicitly developed with the purpose of organizing and representing the specialized knowledge related to the cyber threat space will be presented. In particular, the description will be provided in the perspective of classifying the information characterizing the cyber attacks framework in order to support the interpretation of cyber episodes in a hierarchical way and to enable defense institutions to deal with protection strategies against cyber attacks by knowing their configurations.

2.1 Classification of Cyber Threats

In the field of automatic and predictive detection of cyber threats, multiple studies in the literature of specific interest set the investigative structure on the identification of data functional to the isolation of recursive phenomena that may be related to an imminent cyber threat. In this regard, there are several portals that collate the main cyber attacks occurred over time (Common Attack Pattern Enumerations and Classifications, CAPEC^{TM}), the main vulnerabilities of computer systems (Common Vulnerabilities and Exposures, CVE) and the most affected platforms (Common Platform Enumeration, CPE). Cyber defense practices in the financial-banking sector are particularly widespread (Bhasin 2007[21], Chitra 2013 [33], Al-Janabi 2010 [9], Bsoul, Salim and Zakaria 2013 [28], Lagazio 2014 [75], Jayabrabu 2014 [67], Manpreet 2014 [83], More 2016 [89], Sonaqwanev et al. 2015 [121], Lekha and Prakasam 2017 [78], Begam and Sengottuvelan 2018 [20], Al-Khater et al. 2020 [8], Dubey and Almonayirie 2014 [43]). Specifically, Bhasin (2007) presents an overview of the main fraudulent attack techniques on banking systems, including phishing, the theft of credit card IDs or PINs (Hussein, 2018), iWorms eTrojan horses. The author proposes a list of protection and prevention activities through firewall systems, processes for identifying potential intrusive actions within computer systems or the use of anti-virus and anti-spyware software. Al-Khater et al. (2020) provide a review of cybercrime detection techniques, among which they mention the Cyber terrorism, Child pornography, Cyber espionage, Cyber bullying, Denial of Service, associating each of them with a level of danger and the main targets. The authors report a summary of the main methods based on statistical attack detection mechanisms, such as approaches as the Bayesians, the Markov model etc., as well as implementations on the computational level with Machine Learning techniques, such as KNN, SVM, and Naive bayes algorithms. Begam and Sengottuvelan (2018) study the mechanisms for detecting episodes of banking cyber crime by analyzing a cluster of known attacks relating to this phenomenon for the future recognition of potential attacks. Therefore, the authors present the creation of a database that can serve as a training set for the detection of developing cybercriminal plans. The presented methodology is based on the association of different criminal activities in cyberspace with qualitative values of cybercrime to which weights are associated. Categorized assimilation occurs on the basis

DOI: 10.1201/9781003528999-2

of groups that present vector values to which a high probability of membership can be combined. This process makes it possible to create a cyber crimine archive for prevention studies against cyber attacks and is based on the detection of nominal entities from sector reports and on the analysis of sentences that allow a classification of their role attributes.

For this crime reasoning situation, it can help the experts to distinguish crimes rate analyses with average relative mean cluster and help to settle on speedier choices to reviews the attributes weightage to categorize the crime rates. They crime phrasing a cluster is a gathering of crimes in a topographical locale or a problem area of crime.

Begam and Sengottuvela.2018
Crime Case Reasoning Based Knowledge Discovery Using Sentence Case Relative Clustering for Crime Analyses (pp93)

Bsoul, Salim, and Zakaria (2013) propose a classification approach based on Agglomerative Hierarchical Clustering (by taking into account the importance of the title part in a story) and K-means; Dubey and Almonayirie (2014) report in detail a review of the main classification algorithms used in the financial sector; Sonaqwanev et al. (2015) focus their study on the predictability of crime types through a linear regression approach in order to model the relationships between scalar dependent variables; Lekha and Prakasam (2017) present some data mining models and graphic analysis of crime recursive patterns for the discovery and prediction of cyber attacks from a banking perspective, suggesting the identification of recurrent behaviors by users as approaches for protection and prevention from cyber threats such as association rules and their classification based on decision trees and Influenced Associative Classifier.

From a more semantic perspective, the idea of isolating some focal elements representing illicit or anomalous messages in online language is typical of scientific studies that lead to the detection of typical behaviors on the part of users, or bots, for which it is possible to trace a network of inferential correspondences and understand the basic elements of the recursion of online cyber attacks. There are several moments of scientific-informative meeting based on the sharing of discoveries in the area of cybernetic semantics linked above all to the analysis of offensive uses of web language:

- Workshop on Online abuse and Harms[1] (2019-2020): where (a) Arora et al. (2020) [14] propose the development of machine learning classifiers for identifying the main tactics used by users with offensive intent on Twitter; (b) Ozler et al. (2020) [100] present a methodology for detecting uncivilized language through the use of models based on the Bidirectional Encoder Representations from Transformers (BERT) deep learning model [57] for the classification of cyber harassment activities; (c) Narang and Brew (2010) [94] show the improving characteristics of classifiers based on the syntactic structure of texts and how the dependency graphical convolutional networks (DepGCNs) work better than BERT for real-time detection of offensive messages online; (d) Rathnayake et al. (2020)[109] indicate as an innovative approach for the definition of a semantic modeling of cyberbullying multi-class classification dividing the groups based on roles (victim, offender); (e) Ilan (2020)[20] structures information on the web according to a list of labels representing the offensive use of online language:

---

[1]https://www.workshopononlineabuse.com/

- hostile,
- antagonistic, offensive, provocative/trolling
- hasty
- condescendingly
- sarcastic
- improper generalization.

Each of them is associated with a reliability score with the aim of building a typology of online comments that contribute to creating a climate of hostile conversations between web users; (f) on the same line of research, Kurrek et al. (2020)[73] identify multiple categories of vulgar uses of social language; (g) more specifically aimed at detecting typical events automatically is the study by Shen et al. (2020) [117] which focus on the analysis of events from a pairwise grouping perspective of ¡predicate, main object¿: the relevant predicates are selected, the meaning is disambiguated with the use of a morphosyntactic reference system and typologies are obtained as a result episodic from the merging of the two entities under examination.

- Proceedings of the 4th Workshop on Challenges and Applications of Automated Extraction of Socio-political Events from Text (CASE) 2021[2]: where (a) Re et al. (2021)[110] present an experimental investigation of preventive extraction of possible socio-political conflict events through the implementation of the XLM-RoBERTa model through the consultation of the data contained within the Europe Media Monitor (EMM), a platform which collects in real-time around 300,000 articles from journalistic portals from all over the world in more than 70 languages; (b) Barker et al. (2021)[18] use a model-based approach Natural Language Inference (NLI) used in a textual representation of a target entity that allows to infer the level of salience with which this entity is implicit within the text without the need to be supported by a reference training set.

In the context of studies on the type of characteristic language used for detecting terrorist activities online, Abbasi and Chen (2005)[5] propose a study on the automatic extraction of recurring linguistic values in messages on the web by analyzing the stylistic elements of terrorist semantic schemes in communications. The authors' assessments are the result of an exploratory investigation of the multilingual content of terrorist communications on a global scale. One of the ways in which it has been possible to identify authorship and characterize prototypical traits for each author is the application of the stylometry method. In detail, Abbasi and Chen take into consideration the characteristics of users' writing styles, such as the number of words in a sentence or their distribution, the semantic richness (hapax) and the syntactic and structural characteristics of the text. Among the limitations highlighted are those relating to the length of online messages which, being characterized by a standard number of characters, appear to have less than 100 words, and the diversity of the Arabic language, the object of analysis of their investigation, in the semantic characteristics of the language which can make the process of authorial association within online messages more complex (elements that present a form of diversity compared to Western languages are represented by the rarity of diacritical signs, the brevity of words, the practice of lengthening some points of the text for purely stylistic purposes). Still regarding the study of the characteristic forms of terrorist online language, Omer (2015)[99] proposes an analysis of the typical structure of hashtags in jihadist messages on Twitter, classifying the information according to the id, the date of creation, the text of the tweets, the id of the tweet to which one replies, the id of the user to whom you reply, the screen name of the user you reply

---

[2]https://aclanthology.org/volumes/2021.case-1/

to, and the retweet. The tool used for the purposes of his research is Weka and the classifiers used Support Vector Machine (SVM), Naive Bayes, and AdaBoost. The classification occurs based on the grouping of user information and tweet contents according to the semantic features included within the sentences. Afantenos and Hernandez (2009) [7] present a study on semantic structures within online messages trying to recreate a representative vocabulary then used to identify groups of semantic roles. The latter represents patterns which reflect the content of entities within a particular information context. The authors take into consideration the domain of terrorist acts as a starting context for his exploratory investigation, specifying that: "the intuition behind the messages is the fact that during the evolution of an event there are different activities in progress and each this is in turn broken down into a series of actions. The messages created aim to capture the abstract notion of the actions. Certainly the actions imply, in general terms, different entities. In this case, the entities are represented with the support of a domain ontology. Therefore, a message can be defined as follows:

m = message_type (arg1,..., argn) where argi $\in$ Topic Ontology, i $\in$ {1,...n}

For example, if you are interested in knowing when a plane arrives at its destination or another place, the action can be identified through a message of the "arrives" type whose arguments can be the entity that arrives (plane, vehicle in genre) and the place where it arrives. Arrive (what, place); What: vehicle; Place: Location" (Afantenos and Hernandez.2009).

In summary, the methodology described by Afantenos and Hernandez consists in the creation of a reference lexicon that can quite precisely enclose the candidate messages and semantic roles; the next step involves the use of supervised classification techniques: a word is considered representative of a message if it is used in a sentence annotated with that message, on the contrary it is not taken into consideration. To define the set of messages typical of episodes of terrorist attacks, the study was based on four statistical principles: "frequency of the documentary collection (union of the n% of the most frequent words present in a corpus), documentary frequency (the set which results from the union of the n% most frequent words within each document in the corpus), tfidf (for each of the words in the corpus its tfidf is calculated, then a set is created which is the union of the words with the n % tfidf highest in each document) and internal frequency within documents (a word has an internal frequency within documents if it is present in at least n documents of the corpus)".

Clarke and Grieve (2017) [35] base their research on setting up a method to analyze the predominant characteristics of abusive language on social networks. Specifically, the authors take into consideration Twitter and an approach based on multidimensional analysis (MDA): "[...] using a novel categorical approach to MDA, we have identified 3 dimensions of linguistic variation in racist and sexist Tweets: interactive, antagonistic, and attitudinal. Although there is no absolute distinction between racist and sexist Tweets, by plotting each Tweets dimension coordinates, we have revealed that racist and sexist Tweets do differ functionally in respect to Dimension 2 and Dimension 4, with sexist Tweets tending to be more interactive and attitudinal, perhaps reflecting a somewhat different intent for racist and sexist Tweets" (Clarke and Grieve 2017:8). This type of analysis is based on the relative frequencies of the grammatical functions existing in a given textual grouping which is generally characterized by a fairly high semantic variety. More in detail, the scientific investigation activity is carried out through the use of the library twitteR based on the IDs of some users labeled as sexist or racist in relation to some indicative starting elements such as: lexico-grammatical variants, use of hypertext links, presence of superlative or comparative adjectives. To visualize categorical correspondences the authors propose the use of multiple correspondence analysis (MCA) in R with the FactoMineR library support, and finally the study of dimensional coordinates for the detection of negative polarity in tweets through the use of some determining factors (e.g., the use of the verb to be – which identifies the role of the subject in a noun phrase – numbers, proper names, which guarantee greater specificity with respect to the information given – the use of coordinated and contrastive conjunctions used either to emphasize or to reduce the distance of the expressions present in the sentences). Schmidtz and Wiegand (2017) [115] describe a search based on the extraction of messages with offensive content on the web through the delimitation of some information data such as the insertion of unusual symbols, e.g., ki11, yrslef, or a$$hole, the presence of URLs and punctuation, the length of the tokens, words that cannot be found in English dictionaries, non-alphanumeric characters between the tokens. For the classification of the elements to be analyzed belonging to the vernacular linguistic sphere, the authors indicate the database Ratial slur of the day, while for the presentation of conceptual relations starting from assertions ConceptNet, a tool populated with stereotyped phrases manually extracted from the Formspring social networks (a reference system for studies oriented towards the analysis of hate speech). Caines et al. (2018) [29] base their study on a set of posts published on hacking forums (Gradient boosting classifier XG boost with R). Choshen et al. (2019) [34] are interested in the analysis of the language relating to the illegality of activities on the darknet by comparing the textual contents in clear platforms that present a common thematic trend. The procedure followed for quantifying the differences between the document groups examined starts from the analysis of the words in terms of accuracy and the distribution of the Part of Speech (PoS) tags in the documents. For the identification of nominal entities, the authors use the technique Wikification, which involves connecting the entities with the corresponding article on Wikipedia, while five classifiers were considered to start the classification process: Naive bayes, SVM, Bow, Seq2vec, and Elmo. Yimam et al. (2020)[133] present a research on the definition of an annotation system called "ASAB" (Amharic Sentiment Analysis from Social Media Texts) for a tweet classification model. Through a reference dataset, some metadata were isolated and each tweet was annotated with polarized values "Negative", "Positive", "Neutral", "Mixed". Among the classifiers used there are SVM, KNN, Word2vec, RoBERTa.

2.2 Existing Cyber Threat Classification Models

Cyber threat classification models provide frameworks to identify, categorize, and analyze various cyber threats, vulnerabilities, and attack patterns. These models help in understanding the nature of threats, predicting potential attacks, and devising effective defense mechanisms. Below, key cyber threat classification models will be described, including CVE, CVSS, CWE, CAPEC, MalOnt, Kill Chain Model, and MITRE ATT&CK.

2.2.1 Existing vulnerability classification models

Vulnerability classification models play a crucial role in cybersecurity by standardizing the identification, assessment, and management of software vulnerabilities. These models provide frameworks that help security professionals and organizations understand, communicate about, and mitigate vulnerabilities effectively. Among the most prominent models are CVE, CWE, CPE, and VulnOnt.

2.2.1.1 CVE – Common Vulnerabilities and Exposures

CVE is a publicly available database and identifier system for known cybersecurity vulnerabilities. Each entry, known as a CVE ID, provides a standardized identifier for a specific vulnerability or exposure. This system allows for consistent referencing and sharing of information about vulnerabilities across different security tools and services. CVE entries include an identification number, a description of the vulnerability, and at least one public reference. The CVE List is used in numerous cybersecurity products and services from around the world, including the National Vulnerability Database (NVD), which provides additional analysis and severity rankings based on Common Vulnerability Scoring System (CVSS) scores. CVSS scores are calculated based on several metrics that assess aspects such as the complexity of exploitation, the impact on confidentiality, integrity, and availability, and other environmental factors. Scores range from 0 to 10, with higher scores indicating greater severity.

CVE helps in the standardization of vulnerability information, making it easier for security professionals to quickly understand the nature of a vulnerability, its potential impact, and the necessary steps for mitigation.

2.2.1.2 CWE – Common Weakness Enumeration

CWE is a category system for software and hardware weaknesses and vulnerabilities. It serves as a common language for describing common security weaknesses in code and system architecture, facilitating the identification, mitigation, and prevention of common vulnerabilities. CWE entries describe a software or hardware weakness in a detailed manner, offering examples, related vulnerabilities, and potential mitigations. It provides a comprehensive taxonomy for software weaknesses, enabling better security practices and vulnerability analysis. The CWE catalog contains more than 900 generic software and hardware weakness types. The CWE list organizes weaknesses into categories and views to accommodate different use cases, such as development, testing, architecture, and research. Categories group related weaknesses that share a common characteristic, while views present subsets of the CWE list tailored to specific perspectives or applications.

CWE is widely used in security assessments, code analysis tools, and cybersecurity education to help developers, analysts, and organizations understand and address security weaknesses effectively.

2.2.1.3 CPE – Common Platform Enumeration

CPE is a standardized method of describing and identifying classes of applications, operating systems, and hardware devices within an IT environment. Managed by the National Institute of Standards and Technology (NIST), CPE provides a structured naming scheme for software and hardware products, facilitating the clear and consistent communication of product-specific information across various security tools and databases. CPE identifiers (CPE IDs) are widely used in conjunction with CVE lists and CVSS scoring system. This integration supports efficient vulnerability management and risk assessment processes by linking specific products to known vulnerabilities and their severity scores.

2.2.1.4 VulnOnt – Vulnerability Ontology

VulnOnt is a structured framework designed to classify and analyze cybersecurity vulnerabilities based on their characteristics, behaviors, and impacts. It aims to provide a comprehensive ontology for vulnerabilities, facilitating better analysis, detection, and prevention mechanisms. VulnOnt covers various aspects of vulnerabilities, including the type of software flaws, the attack vectors, the potential impacts, and the required conditions for exploitation. This ontology supports the semantic web technology, enabling automated reasoning about vulnerabilities and their relationships.

By providing a more detailed classification and understanding of vulnerabilities, VulnOnt aids in the development of more sophisticated security tools and methodologies for vulnerability management and threat assessment.

2.2.2   Existing attack patterns classification models

Attack pattern classification models are frameworks or systems designed to categorize, describe, and communicate the various methods, strategies, and techniques attackers use to exploit vulnerabilities, compromise systems, and achieve their objectives. These models provide structured ways to categorize and analyze the behaviors, strategies, and techniques used by cyber adversaries. They help cybersecurity professionals to understand threats, develop defenses, and share information about cyberattacks more effectively.

2.2.2.1   CAPEC – Common Attack Pattern Enumeration and Classification

CAPEC provides a comprehensive dictionary of known attack patterns that adversaries use to exploit known vulnerabilities in cyber systems. It is designed to facilitate the discussion, understanding, and research of adversarial tactics and techniques. CAPEC entries include a description of the attack, prerequisites for its execution, the attack's execution flow, and potential mitigations. They are associated with weaknesses (linked to CWE entries), and possible mitigations. It serves as a tool for educators, software developers, testers, and security practitioners to better understand and defend against cyber attacks.

2.2.2.2   MalOnt – Malware Ontology

MalOnt is focused on classifying malware based on their behavior, characteristics, and attack methods. It provides a structured framework to categorize malware into different families and types, enabling better analysis and understanding of malware threats. MalOnt aids in malware detection and analysis by providing a detailed ontology that can be used for training machine learning models or for systematic malware research and classification.

2.2.2.3   MAEC – Malware Attribute Enumeration and Characterization

MAEC is a standardized language for encoding and communicating information about malware based on its attributes and behaviors. Similar to CAPEC, MAEC focuses specifically on classifying and describing malware instances and their attack patterns. It captures details about malware such as behaviors, artifacts, attack patterns, and relationships with other malware, providing a structured framework for malware analysis and defense.

2.2.2.4   Kill Chain Model

The Cyber Kill Chain framework, developed by Lockheed Martin, describes the phases of a cyber attack from early reconnaissance to the final action on objectives. This model helps organizations understand and defend against cyber attacks by breaking down the attack process into manageable segments, allowing for the identification and blocking of adversaries at different stages.

The kill chain model breaks down into seven distinct phases:

1. Reconnaissance: In this initial phase, attackers gather information on their target to identify vulnerabilities, entry points, and valuable assets. Methods can include public domain searches, social engineering, and network scanning.

2. Weaponization: The attacker creates a malware-loaded weapon, such as a virus or worm, tailored to exploit the vulnerabilities identified in the reconnaissance phase. This weapon is crafted to deliver the payload without detection.

3. Delivery: The weaponized bundle is delivered to the target via email phishing, malicious websites, USB devices, or other methods. The goal is to trick the user or system into executing the malicious payload.

4. Exploitation: Upon successful delivery, the malicious payload exploits a vulnerability within the target's system to execute its code. This phase marks the initial compromise of the system.

5. Installation: The exploitation phase leads to the installation of malware on the victim's system, allowing the attacker sustained access to the network. Malware may also establish backdoors for future access.

6. Command and Control (C2): The installed malware establishes a command and control channel back to the attacker, allowing them to remotely control the compromised system and exfiltrate data, deploy additional malware, or issue commands.

7. Actions on Objectives: With control established, the attackers execute their final objective, which could include data theft, data destruction, espionage, or preparing for additional attacks.

2.2.2.5   MITRE ATT&CK: Tactics and Techniques

The MITRE ATT&CK framework is a comprehensive matrix of tactics and techniques used by threat actors throughout the various stages of an information security incident. It serves as a knowledge base for cybersecurity and provides a structured classification system to describe the actions an adversary may take while operating within a network. The core concepts within the MITRE ATT&CK framework are the following:

- **Tactics**: These represent the "why" of an ATT&CK technique or the adversary's objective. Tactics are the overarching goals that attackers are trying to achieve in the context of their cyber operations, such as gaining initial access, executing commands, persisting through defenses, and exfiltrating data.

- **Techniques**: These are the "how" of the ATT&CK model, describing the methods adversaries use to achieve tactical objectives. Techniques provide specific details on the actions adversaries may take to accomplish their goals, such as phishing for initial access, using PowerShell for execution, or data encryption for impact.

- **Sub-techniques**: Some techniques have further details provided in sub-techniques, which offer a more granular view of the methods used by adversaries. Sub-techniques break down the parent technique into more specific actions that an adversary might take.

The ATT&CK framework is divided into several domains, each focusing on a different aspect of cybersecurity for specific environments:

- Enterprise: Covers techniques used against enterprise networks, cloud environments, and mobile devices.

- Mobile: Focuses specifically on tactics and techniques relevant to mobile platforms.

- ICS (Industrial Control Systems): Addresses techniques that affect industrial control systems and operational technology environments.

TABLE 2.1

Summary of key MITRE ATT&CK tactics.

Tactic	Description
Initial Access	Techniques for gaining entry into a network, such as phishing and exploiting public-facing applications.
Execution	Methods by which malicious code is executed on a victim's system, for example, through scripting or command interpreters.
Persistence	Techniques ensuring the adversaries maintain their foothold despite disruptions.
Privilege Escalation	Methods to gain higher-level permissions on a system or network.
Defense Evasion	Techniques used to avoid detection, such as disabling security software and obfuscating malicious files.
Credential Access	Tactics for stealing credentials to facilitate unauthorized access.
Discovery	Techniques used to gain knowledge about the system, network, and environment.
Lateral Movement	Methods used to move through a network in search of key assets and data.
Collection	Gathering data of interest to the adversary's goals.
Command and Control	Methods for communicating with compromised systems to control them remotely.
Exfiltration	Techniques for stealing data and extracting it from the target network.
Impact	Tactics aimed at disrupting, destroying, or manipulating systems and data.

Table 2.1 presents a summary of key MITRE ATT&CK tactics, outlining their primary focus and providing examples where applicable. It is designed to serve as a quick reference to understand the tactics used by adversaries in cyber attacks. The ATT&CK Framework is constantly evolving and consists of more than 150 techniques and 270 sub-techniques divided into 14 tactics. It outlines the full lifecycle of a cyber attack, from initial access through to actions on objectives, such as data exfiltration or encryption in the case of ransomware. This lifecycle view helps organizations understand how attackers operate and the steps they take to achieve their goals. For each tactic (an attacker's goal), the framework lists specific techniques (how the goal is achieved), offering detailed insights into attacker methods. Understanding these techniques allows defenders to spot early indicators of ransomware activity, such as techniques for initial access (phishing, exploiting vulnerabilities) or execution (scripting, user execution).

The MITRE ATT&CK framework is a valuable resource for understanding the strategies and methods used by threat actors. By analyzing incidents through the lens of ATT&CK, organizations can better prepare for, and respond to, cyberattacks. By mapping security controls against ATT&CK techniques, organizations can identify potential gaps in their defenses that ransomware or other malware might exploit. This gap analysis is crucial for prioritizing security improvements. It also helps in the development of detection rules and response strategies. For ransomware, this might include detecting the use of file encryption utilities or the modification of backup files. Further more, it allows the profiling of known threat groups, including those that deploy ransomware, based on observed tactics and techniques. This profiling aids in anticipating the strategies a given group might employ in future attacks. It provides a common language for the cybersecurity community to share threat intelligence. Organizations can leverage this shared knowledge to better defend against specific ransomware strains or adapt to emerging threats.

Cyber Kill Chain vs. MITRE ATT&CK

The Cyber Kill Chain and the MITRE ATT&CK framework are both models used to describe and analyze cyber threats, but they approach the task from different perspectives and serve slightly different purposes. The main key differences between them are the following:

- Scope and detail: The Kill Chain model provides a high-level overview of the stages of an attack, focusing on external penetration into a network. ATT&CK offers a more granular view of attacker tactics and techniques, including a wider variety of behaviors that occur both before and after initial access is gained.

- Linearity: The Kill Chain follows a linear progression, which assumes that disrupting one stage can stop the attack. In contrast, ATT&CK recognizes the complexity of modern attacks, which may not follow a strictly linear path and can involve multiple tactics and techniques at various stages.

- Post-compromise focus: While the Kill Chain emphasizes preventing breaches, ATT&CK focuses extensively on what happens after an attacker has gained access, providing detailed information on how to detect and respond to actions attackers take within the network.

- Versatility and use cases: The Kill Chain model is particularly useful for preventing attacks, while ATT&CK's detailed breakdown of tactics and techniques makes it invaluable for a broader range of purposes, including detection, response, and threat intelligence analysis.

During a ransomware incident, this framework can guide analysts in identifying attacker actions, understanding their impact, and formulating an effective response. This structured approach ensures that critical steps are not overlooked in the situation of an incident. By understanding the tactics and techniques, organizations can adopt a more proactive security posture, implementing measures like network segmentation, application whitelisting, and rigorous access controls to mitigate the risk of ransomware attacks.

2.2.3 Existing Cybersecurity Knowledge Graphs (CKG)

In the literature the works aimed at proposing knowledge bases to structure the information about cyber threats have been drawing an extended interest. As a matter of fact, Keshavarzi and Gharrafy (2023) [70] point out how increasingly urgent it has become to have a set of knowledge structuring systems facing the constant development in ransomware assaults, and propose an ontology configuration called *Rantology* representing the information around the digital to extortion attacks, by isolating just the Windows ransomware. Specifically targeted to ransomware formalization works, Ariffin et al. (2018) [13] propose a ransomware knowledge base construction using unstructured user-generated textual data like forum resulting in an ontology of digital blackmails, focusing on ransomware assaults and using a six-layers data to enrich the ransomware knowledge base derived from malware threat lists and reports, i.e., "Name: The name of different Ransomware family; Aliases: Variant name of Ransomware; Type: Category of Ransomware family belongs to; Discover date: The data of

Ransomware being discovered; Target: The system or any application affected or targeted by the Ransomware; Infection vector: Method or platform used by Ransomware to spread" (2018:2). Recent works on ransomware classification have been published based on the implementation of multiple machine learning algorithms [8] or static analysis by transforming the opcode sequences of ransomware into N-grams [136]. Cybersecurity knowledge graphs and frameworks [118] provide structured representations of cyber threat data, relationships, and intelligence. They facilitate a deeper understanding of threats, vulnerabilities, and attack patterns, aiding in cybersecurity defense strategies. The construction of CKGs usually starts with developing a cybersecurity ontology, from which semantic triples are extracted to form the backbone of the knowledge graph. This approach is widely adopted across studies aiming to provide a structured and semantically rich representation of cybersecurity information [137].

Recent advancements in CKG development have focused on discovering hidden cybersecurity patterns through hierarchical clustering, highlighting the technologies frequently exploited in cyber-attacks [41]. Moreover, innovative methodologies, such as utilizing machine learning to build ontology and extract entities for CKGs, have been proposed, showcasing the dynamic evolution of CKG construction techniques [68]. Additionally, comprehensive reviews of CKG application scenarios offer insights into the practical applications and the future direction of research, emphasizing the importance of addressing current research flaws and exploring new methodologies [80].

2.2.3.1   STIX: Structured Threat Information eXpression

STIX is a language and serialization format used for sharing cyber threat intelligence (CTI). Developed by MITRE and now managed by OASIS, STIX enables organizations to communicate about cyber threats in a consistent and machine-readable format. It is designed to improve the prevention, detection, and mitigation of cyber threats on a global scale. It is comprised of multiple components that describe various aspects of cyber threat intelligence. These components include Indicators, Tactics, Techniques, and Procedures (TTPs), Campaigns, Threat Actors, Incidents, Vulnerabilities, and Observables. Each component serves a specific purpose, from detailing the behavior of threat actors to describing observed data that may indicate a cyber attack.

At the heart of STIX are objects known as STIX Domain Objects (SDOs) and STIX Relationship Objects (SROs). SDOs represent the core concepts and entities involved in cyber threat intelligence, while SROs define the relationships between these entities. This structure not only captures detailed information about threats but also the context in which they operate, enhancing the overall understanding of the threat landscape.

The power of STIX lies in its ability to facilitate the sharing of threat intelligence across different platforms, tools, and organizations. By adopting a common language for threat information, entities can efficiently exchange data on emerging threats, ongoing attacks, and observed tactics, reducing the time it takes for critical intelligence to reach those who can act on it. This interoperability is further supported by TAXII (Trusted Automated Exchange of Indicator Information), a protocol designed for the secure exchange of STIX data.

2.2.3.2   SEPSES Cybersecurity Knowledge Graph

The SEPSES Cybersecurity Knowledge Graph is a comprehensive framework designed to integrate, model, and semantically link a wide range of cybersecurity data and intelligence sources. Developed to address the challenges of data silos and the lack of interoperability among cybersecurity information systems, SEPSES aims to provide a unified, queryable, and extensible platform for cybersecurity analytics, threat detection, and decision support.

EPSES ingests data on vulnerabilities, weaknesses, and attack patterns from various publicly available sources. By harmonizing this information within a single knowledge graph, SEPSES facilitates a holistic view of the cybersecurity landscape.

At the core of SEPSES is the use of semantic web technologies and ontologies including OWL and RDF, which allow the modeling of complex relationships between different data entities. The knowledge graph structure enables users to perform sophisticated queries using SPARQL across linked data points, uncovering insights that might be difficult to obtain from traditional, disconnected datasets. Analysts can explore attack patterns, trace threat origins, and identify potential vulnerabilities across systems with greater efficiency.

2.2.3.3 MITRE CyGraph

CyGraph is a cybersecurity graph analytics tool developed by the MITRE Corporation. It leverages graph theory and analytics to model, analyze, and visualize complex cybersecurity data and relationships within an organization's network. CyGraph aims to provide a comprehensive understanding of an organization's cyber risk posture by mapping out networks, vulnerabilities, assets, and potential attack paths. It uses graph-based representations to depict networks and their components, including devices, users, applications, and data. This model allows the visualization of connections and dependencies within the network infrastructure. It integrates data on known vulnerabilities (e.g., from CVEs and other vulnerability databases) with the network model to identify potential security weaknesses that could be exploited by attackers.

One of CyGraph's core functionalities is to calculate and visualize possible attack paths through a network. This analysis helps identifying how an attacker could potentially move laterally through the network to reach critical assets. By analyzing the network model, vulnerabilities, and potential attack paths, CyGraph can assess the overall cyber risk facing an organization. It helps prioritizing risks based on the potential impact and likelihood of exploitation.

CyGraph provides a situational awareness of the cybersecurity landscape within an organization. It highlights critical assets, potential vulnerabilities, and how various parts of the network are interconnected and could be impacted by cyber attacks. The insights gained from CyGraph can inform incident response and recovery efforts, guiding strategic decisions on how to mitigate vulnerabilities, respond to incidents, and recover from attacks.

2.2.3.4 UCO: Unified Cybersecurity Ontology

The Unified Cybersecurity Ontology (UCO) is a structured framework designed to standardize the representation and integration of cybersecurity information across various domains and sources. By providing a common vocabulary and set of relationships for cybersecurity entities, UCO aims to enhance the interoperability, sharing, and analysis of cybersecurity data, facilitating more effective threat intelligence, incident response, and security operations. UCO encompasses a broad range of cybersecurity concepts, including threats, vulnerabilities, incidents, and countermeasures. It aligns these concepts in a coherent structure, enabling clear communication and understanding among cybersecurity professionals and systems.

Utilizing semantic web technologies, UCO models complex relationships between cybersecurity entities, supporting advanced queries and analytics. This semantic linking allows for the exploration of intricate patterns and connections within cybersecurity data, contributing to deeper insights and more informed decision-making.

The ontology's structured approach of UCO not only aids in the organization and classification of cybersecurity information but also supports automated reasoning and inference. This capability enables the identification of implicit relationships and the derivation of new knowledge from existing data, further augmenting cybersecurity analysis and threat detection efforts.

2.2.3.5   TAGraph: Knowledge Graph of Threat Actor

The TAGraph is a framework designed to create a knowledge graph of threat actors by building an ontology of threat actors and employing a named entity recognition system to extract cybersecurity-related entities. This innovative approach addresses the challenge of understanding the cybersecurity threat landscape, particularly information about threat actors, which is typically hidden and scattered across various sources. Online news has emerged as a popular and critical source of information for cybersecurity professionals to learn about the activities conducted by these threat actors. By leveraging the TAGraph framework, it is possible to automatically extract cybersecurity-related entities from articles and construct a knowledge graph of threat actors, thus enabling a more structured and comprehensive understanding of their behaviors and patterns.

TAGraph builds an Ontology of Threat Actors to provide a structured and formal representation of the knowledge concerning threat actors. This ontology defines the concepts within the domain and the relationships between those concepts, facilitating a systematic approach to capturing and organizing information about threat actors. A NER system is designed to identify and classify key information in text into predefined categories. In the context of TAGraph, the named entity recognition system specifically targets cybersecurity-related entities, such as threat actors, attack types, vulnerabilities, and affected systems. By recognizing these entities, the system can extract relevant information from unstructured text sources like online news articles. Utilizing the extracted entities and the relationships defined in the ontology, TAGraph constructs a knowledge graph that visualizes the connections between threat actors and their activities. This graph serves as a powerful tool for cybersecurity analysts, allowing them to explore complex relationships and gain insights into the threat landscape.

The knowledge graph generated by TAGraph supports various cybersecurity tasks, including threat intelligence analysis, security incident investigation, and strategic planning for defense. By providing a detailed and interconnected view of threat actors and their actions, TAGraph aids in identifying patterns, predicting potential threats, and devising effective countermeasures.

2.2.3.6   STUCCO

The STUCCO project[3] developed an ontology to organize and schema information for a cybersecurity knowledge graph database. Their initiative aims to integrate information from various structured and unstructured data sources within the cybersecurity domain, providing a structured framework that encompasses all relevant concepts. STUCCO integrates data from a variety of sources, including antivirus (AV) vendors, DNS requests, and network traffic information by using 115 properties to characterize them and their relationships. It addresses the inconsistency and lack of detailed information across these sources, aiming for a more unified data resource.

The ontology includes a wide variety of publicly available datasets, as well as internal information like netflows and IDS alerts. It is designed to represent the information in a useful manner for both analysts and automated tools, considering the constraints of available datasets. It is specified using JSON-Schema, compatible with the GraphSON format used in graph databases like Titan. This choice simplifies data validation and defines the database schema but lacks certain capabilities like automatic reasoning available in OWL.

---

[3]https://stucco.github.io/

2.2.3.7 MITRE D3FEND™

MITRE D3FEND[4] is a framework developed by MITRE, designed to complement the already established MITRE ATT&CK framework. While ATT&CK provides a detailed understanding of adversary tactics and techniques based on real-world observations, D3FEND focuses on countermeasures, aimed at defending against the specific tactics and techniques documented in ATT&CK.

The D3FEND framework introduces a knowledge graph that catalogs and details various cybersecurity defense tactics and techniques. These techniques are structured to mirror the attack methods outlined in ATT&CK, thereby providing a direct correlation between attack types and their corresponding defensive strategies. The graph was informed by an analysis of numerous sources, including a targeted review of over 500 countermeasure patents from the U.S. Patent Office spanning from 2001 to 2018. The relations between offensive and defensive models are using the digital artifacts to map defensive capabilities against offensive tactics, techniques, and procedures (TTPs). These artifacts are defined using the Digital Artifact Ontology (DAO) specifying the concepts necessary to classify and represent digital objects relevant to cybersecurity analysis. Artifacts may be simple or compound, with the potential to comprise other artifacts. This hierarchical structure allows for the representation of complex digital entities and their interrelations. The DAO is designed to be abstract and semantic, focusing on the representation of digital artifacts beyond vendor-specific or purely syntactic descriptions. This abstraction enables inferential reasoning and a unified representation across different cybersecurity contexts. D3FEND uses the digital artifacts defined in the DAO to link defensive techniques directly to the digital artifacts associated with offensive TTPs. This linkage is critical for effectively countering specific cyber threats. The identified relationship allows cybersecurity professionals to navigate from known attack tactics directly to potential defenses, enhancing the practical applicability of both frameworks in a synergistic manner. By understanding the relationships between different digital artifacts and the techniques that produce, execute, analyze, access, or install them, cybersecurity analysts can infer defensive strategies without needing to manually relate every offensive technique to a specific countermeasure.

The knowledge graph within D3FEND is designed to be comprehensive and navigable, offering detailed metadata about each defensive technique, including its effectiveness, implementation considerations, and how it interacts with other techniques within the ecosystem. This structured approach not only helps in identifying suitable defenses but also in understanding the broader context of cybersecurity strategies. The framework delineates these into specific tactics and techniques, each designed to address different aspects of cyber threats.

D3FEND categorizes defense into several overarching tactics, each representing a general class of action taken in response to adversarial activities. These tactics include:

- **Model**: Applying security engineering, vulnerability, threat, and risk analyzes to digital systems.

- **Detect**: Identifying and recognizing adversarial actions or anomalies within the system.

- **Harden**: Strengthening systems to reduce vulnerabilities and increase resistance to attacks.

- **Deceive**: Implementing measures that mislead attackers about the system's actual characteristics or operations.

- **Evict**: Removing adversaries from the system once they are detected.

---

[4]https://d3fend.mitre.org/

- **Isolate**: Segregating parts of the network or system to contain the damage and prevent the spread of malicious activities.

- **Restore**: Returning the system to a better state.

These tactics serve as the most general organizing classes within the D3FEND knowledge graph and are action-oriented, carefully selected to generalize multiple techniques under each category. Beneath these tactics, D3FEND defines more specific techniques, which are the actual methods employed to realize the tactics. The techniques are represented hierarchically under each tactic in the knowledge graph, forming a taxonomy from the most general to the most specific. This hierarchical arrangement helps in understanding the interrelationships and specific applications of each technique within broader defensive strategies.

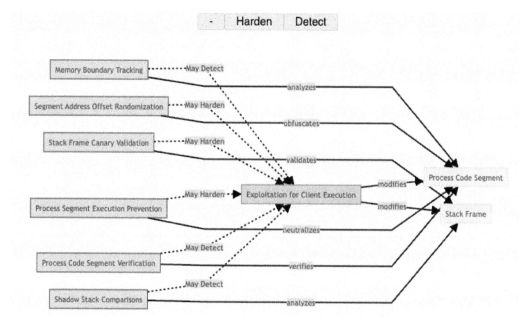

FIGURE 2.1

A mapping between the attack technique Exploitation for Client Execution (T1203) and its respective defense tactics and techniques using the MITRE D3DEFEND™ framework. Source: https://d3fend.mitre.org/offensive-technique/attack/T1203/.

An example of a mapping between the MITRE ATT&CK technique Exploitation for Client Execution (T1203), where an attacker tries to execute arbitrary code on a client's system, and its respective defense tactics and techniques is depicted in Figure 2.1. The mapping is done through two digital artifacts which are Process Code Segment and Stack Frame, where each of them can be modified by the attack technique T1203. Two defense tactics, i.e., Harden and Detect, can be applied to mitigate this attack technique through defense techniques including Memory Boundary Tracking, Process Code Segment Verification, Shadow Stack Comparisons for detection, and Segment Address Offset Randomization, Stack Frame Canary Validation, Process Segment Execution Prevention for Hardening. The solid arrows linking defense technique and attack technique through the digital artifacts contain the mitigation actions like "obfuscates", "validates", and "neutralizes", to avoid the exploitation of the technique by an attacker.

The D3FEND knowledge graph visualizes these tactics and techniques in a tabular view that accounts for their hierarchical relationships, shown in the user interface as a directed, acyclic graph. Each element within this graph links to more detailed information about the technique, enabling users to delve deeper into how each technique operates and its relevance to specific cybersecurity challenges. The structure of D3FEND allows defenders to trace the flow from high-level defensive maneuvers (tactics) down to specific actionable methods (techniques). This not only aids in strategic planning against cyber threats but also enhances the understanding of how different defensive measures interconnect to form a comprehensive defense strategy. These tactics and techniques form the core of D3FEND's approach to organizing and representing cybersecurity knowledge, enabling it to provide a systematic, reasoned approach to cyber defense based on understanding the relationships between techniques and the digital artifacts associated with them. This structure supports inferential reasoning and strategic deployment of cybersecurity measures, tailored to effectively counter identified threats.

By integrating D3FEND with ATT&CK, organizations can achieve a more balanced view of cyber threats and defenses, facilitating proactive security planning and response. This integration is pivotal for developing robust cybersecurity policies and operations that are informed by a thorough understanding of both how attackers operate and how defenders can effectively counteract.

3

Building a Ransomware Knowledge Base

In this chapter the process of building the source corpus will be presented. A first part will be dedicated ransomware case studies focusing on the four major ransomware and early attempts. Subsequently the Chapter presents a preliminary introduction on documentation representativeness and the importance of relying on authoritative types of documentation to start the information retrieval process on a specific subject, in this case the association of ransomware with the vulnerabilities in order to provide a means through which a prediction of future cyber attacks can be possible to achieve. The second part will cover the specificity of the corpus compiled for the purposes of this research activity expanding on the features characterizing the documentation under analysis and the granularity of information contained in it meant to be studied for the extraction of the main concepts related to the knowledge framework of ransomware.

3.1 Ransomware Case Studies

In this section, we present major ransomware cases to mainly show their operating mode and their impact on different types of organizations. For each case study, we analyze the vulnerabilities and the attack techniques and tactics used by the ransomware. We also focus on their evolution over years regarding their level of sophistication and the targeted organizations. This analysis provides first insights about ransomware behaviors and assists in their family attribution. Four major ransomware cases have been chosen to mainly show the pathway from early ransomware attempts to the present-day sophisticated ransomware attacks [97].

3.1.1 Early ransomware attempts

Early ransomware attempts date back to the late 1980s, with notable distinctions from the sophisticated ransomware strains we see today in terms of complexity, propagation methods, and impact. These initial attempts were relatively primitive, leveraging basic encryption methods or simply locking users out of their systems without actually encrypting files. A representative set of early and known ransomware attempts is hereby provided:

- AIDS trojan also known as PC Cyborg (1989): The AIDS Trojan is considered one of the first examples of ransomware. It was distributed via floppy disks labeled as containing information on the AIDS virus, intended for attendees of the World Health Organization's AIDS conference. Once a computer ran the software on the disk, the Trojan would count the number of times the computer was booted. After the 90th reboot, it would hide directories and encrypt the names of all files on the C drive, rendering the system unusable. The ransom note directed victims to send \$189 to a PO Box in Panama to recover their

DOI: 10.1201/9781003528999-3

files, though it used symmetric encryption, and technical users could reverse the process without paying.

- Archievus (early 2000s): Archievus was one of the early ransomware that encrypted files. It targeted and encrypted files in the "My Documents" folder on Windows systems using a simple symmetric encryption algorithm. It was distributed through malware downloads and phishing emails. It displayed a message demanding payment for a decryption key. However, due to its relatively simple encryption method, tools were quickly developed to decrypt the files without paying the ransom.

- Gpcode (Mid-2000s, with several variants appearing up until around 2010): Gpcode was more advanced than its predecessors. It used RSA encryption, a significant step up in complexity, making it harder to decrypt files without the key. Each variant of Gpcode came with a stronger encryption key, with the last known variant using a 1024-bit key. It spreads via malicious email attachments and exploited websites. The ransom note included an email address through which the victim could negotiate the ransom and receive instructions on making a payment in exchange for the decryption key.

Early ransomware attempts have major differences from modern ransomware. They often used simple or flawed encryption methods, making it possible for security researchers to crack them and recover files without paying the ransom. Modern ransomware uses robust encryption algorithms like AES and RSA, making decryption practically impossible without the unique key.

While early ransomware spreads through physical media (like floppy disks) or basic digital methods (email attachments), modern variants use sophisticated techniques, including exploit kits, phishing campaigns, and leveraging vulnerabilities in network systems for widespread infection.

The digitalization of payment systems was also a vector of development of ransomware. By analogy, those were boosters for the adoption of e-commerce and also for cyber-criminal activities including ransomware among others. Early attempts had rudimentary payment demands aligned the existing solutions at that time, often involving postal mail or wire transfers. Modern ransomware can leverage recent techniques for money exchange and particularly use cryptocurrencies for ransom payments, providing anonymity to the attackers.

Initially, ransomware targeted individual users or small networks. Today, ransomware attacks can cripple entire organizations, national or local authorities, and critical infrastructure with a global impact.

3.1.2 CryptoLocker

Marking a significant evolution in ransomware, CryptoLocker emerged in 2013 as one of the first ransomware to use sophisticated encryption methods to lock users' files. It demanded payment in Bitcoin for the decryption key, leveraging the anonymity of cryptocurrency to evade law enforcement. CryptoLocker's success inspired numerous variants and set a new standard for ransomware attacks, emphasizing the use of strong encryption and ransom payments in cryptocurrency.

Initially, CryptoLocker primarily targeted Windows operating systems on both individual and organizational levels. It focused on personal documents, images, and other valuable files that would compel victims to pay the ransom. While there was no specific geographic targeting, incidents were heavily reported in the United States and several European countries. Organizations across various sectors, including healthcare, academia, and small businesses, were affected due to the indiscriminate nature of the attacks.

CryptoLocker used a combination of RSA and AES encryption. It generated a unique AES key for encrypting files on the victim's computer, which was then encrypted with a

RSA public key generated by the attackers' server. This ensured that only the holder of the RSA private key could decrypt the AES key used on the victim's files. It specifically targeted files with extensions that are typically associated with work documents, pictures, and databases, such as .doc, .xls, .pdf, and .jpg, among others.

One common method of distribution was through exploit kits on compromised websites, where vulnerabilities in the browser or its plugins (like Java, Adobe Flash, and Adobe Reader) were exploited to install CryptoLocker without user interaction. It also relies on phishing emails with malicious attachments as a major vector. These emails are often masqueraded as legitimate communications containing executable files disguised as PDFs or office documents. The use of existing botnets, particularly Gameover ZeuS, was a significant factor in CryptoLocker's spread. Infected systems within this botnet were used to distribute the ransomware further via spam campaigns.

Although CryptoLocker's primary operation did not include data exfiltration, the sheer threat of permanent data loss pressured victims into paying the ransom. This tactic laid the groundwork for future ransomware attacks incorporating data theft and double extortion. Victims were typically given a deadline (e.g., 72 hours) to pay the ransom, often demanded in Bitcoin to maintain anonymity. The ransom amount varied, with reports ranging from a few hundred to several thousand dollars. Victims were instructed to use Tor to access the payment portal, further anonymizing the attackers' operations. After payment, the decryption key was reportedly provided in most cases, allowing victims to recover their files. In a somewhat novel approach at the time, the attackers offered a decryption service, providing a website where victims could upload an encrypted file to verify the ability to decrypt it after payment.

CryptoLocker was remarkably successful, infecting an estimated 500,000 to over a million systems and generating millions in ransom payments before law enforcement agencies and security companies disrupted its operation in mid-2014. The response involved taking down the Gameover ZeuS botnet and seizing servers associated with CryptoLocker, ultimately helping to decrypt many affected systems. The legacy of CryptoLocker is significant, as it demonstrated the lucrative potential of ransomware to cybercriminals and paved the way for more sophisticated and damaging strains like WannaCry, NotPetya, and others.

3.1.3   WannaCry

In May 2017, WannaCry caused unprecedented disruption by exploiting vulnerabilities in Microsoft Windows operating systems. Its rapid spread across networks made it one of the most notorious ransomware attacks in history. WannaCry demonstrated the potential for ransomware to cause global impact. It is one of the most widespread and damaging cyberattacks in history, affecting more than 230,000 computers across over 150 countries. The ransomware targeted a wide range of sectors, including healthcare, finance, and government, causing significant operational and financial damage.

WannaCry did not discriminate in its targets, affecting both individual users and large organizations. However, its impact was particularly severe in organizations with outdated or unpatched Windows systems. Several high-profile organizations were affected, including the National Health Service (NHS) in the UK, where it caused the cancellation of medical procedures and appointments, Spanish telecommunications company Telefónica, and numerous other entities worldwide.

WannaCry used AES and RSA encryption algorithms to encrypt files on the infected system. It targeted specific file types, including documents, images, and databases, appending them with the ".WCRY" file extension. Victims were presented with a ransom note demanding payment in Bitcoin for the decryption key. The ransom amount initially demanded was $300, which doubled after a set period if not paid. There was also a countdown timer threatening the deletion of files if the ransom was not paid within a week.

The primary vector for WannaCry's rapid spread was the exploitation of a vulnerability in Microsoft's Server Message Block (SMB) protocol. This vulnerability, known as Eternal-Blue, was initially discovered by the U.S. National Security Agency (NSA) and leaked by the Shadow Brokers group. Microsoft had released a patch (MS17-010) before the attack, but many systems remained unpatched and vulnerable. This vulnerability actually affects windows version from XP to 8.1 and is mainly due to the possibility for an unauthenticated user, the attacker, to send malformed SMB packets leading to a buffer overflow. As a result, binary code is written and executed on the victim. This code actually runs a backdoor, called DoublePulsar, allowing remote malicious interaction through SMB protocol.

Unlike traditional ransomware, which relies on phishing or manual installation by attackers, WannaCry spread autonomously across networks. After infecting one machine, it used the EternalBlue exploit to find and infect other vulnerable machines within the network and on the internet, contributing to its rapid global spread. A unique aspect of WannaCry was the inclusion of a kill switch. The malware would attempt to connect to a specific, unregistered domain before proceeding with its operations. A security researcher accidentally halted the initial outbreak by registering this domain, effectively activating the kill switch and preventing further infections from spreading. WannaCry's implementation of its ransom payment system was relatively unsophisticated. It did not use unique Bitcoin addresses for each victim, making it difficult for the attackers to verify who had paid the ransom, leading to challenges in the decryption process for those who paid.

NotPetya is another ransomware taking benefit from the EternalBlue vulnerability but is also capable to use alternatively another SMB vulnerability, EternalRomance. Actually, like WannaCry, the first objective is to install the backdoor. In both cases, the presence of the backdoor is checked to avoid trying to reinfect already infected victims during malware spread. However, WannaCry and NotPetya differ by the type of message exchanged to perform this check.

The WannaCry outbreak led to significant financial and operational impacts worldwide, with estimated damages ranging from hundreds of millions to billions of dollars. The attack highlighted the critical importance of regular system updates and patches, especially for critical vulnerabilities. It also sparked debates on the ethics and risks associated with government agencies stockpiling knowledge of software vulnerabilities. In response, Microsoft released emergency patches for even unsupported versions of Windows to protect against WannaCry, emphasizing the severity of the threat.

3.1.4   Ryuk

First identified in 2018, Ryuk represents the trend towards targeted ransomware attacks against high-value and specific organizations, often with demands for significantly higher ransoms. Unlike earlier, more opportunistic ransomware, Ryuk targets are carefully selected, and the attacks are meticulously planned to maximize disruption and increase the likelihood of a substantial ransom payment. This evolution towards targeted attacks signifies the growing sophistication of ransomware development.

Ryuk has primarily targeted organizations in sectors such as healthcare, government, finance, and critical infrastructures. Its attacks are known for being highly selective, focusing on entities that are likely to pay large sums to regain access to their critical data. Despite its selective nature, Ryuk has affected organizations worldwide, indicating that the actors behind it are not limited by geography in their targeting.

Ryuk uses a combination of symmetric (AES) and asymmetric (RSA) encryption algorithms. It encrypts files on the infected system with AES, and then the AES key itself is encrypted with an RSA public key. This ensures that only the attacker, who possesses the corresponding RSA private key, can decrypt the affected files. Ryuk selectively encrypts files that are critical to business operations, including databases, document storage, and other key operational files. It is known to delete volume shadow copies on Windows to prevent file recovery via Windows backup utilities.

Ryuk attackers often gain initial access through spear-phishing emails, exploiting remote desktop protocol (RDP) vulnerabilities, or by leveraging credentials stolen from other malware infections such as TrickBot or Emotet. Once inside a network, the attackers typically use common penetration testing tools and techniques to move laterally, escalate privileges, and map out the network to identify valuable targets for encryption.

Unlike many ransomware strains that spread automatically, Ryuk attacks often involve a hands-on approach from the attackers. After gaining access and exploring the network, attackers manually deploy Ryuk on identified valuable systems. Ryuk is known for its ability to identify and disable or delete network backups, making recovery more difficult for the victims and increasing the likelihood of the ransom being paid. The ransom notes left by Ryuk demand payment in Bitcoin, with the amounts often tailored to the size and perceived ability to pay off the victim organization. Ransoms demanded by Ryuk have been some of the highest observed in ransomware attacks.

The Ryuk ransomware represents a significant threat to organizations due to its targeted nature, sophistication, and the manual involvement of attackers. Organizations affected by Ryuk have experienced substantial financial losses, not just from the ransom payments but also due to operational downtime and recovery costs.

3.1.5   Lockbit

LockBit is a ransomware-as-a-service (RaaS) operation known for its highly efficient encryption methods and for targeting a wide range of industries worldwide. Since its emergence in September 2019, LockBit has evolved through several iterations, with LockBit 2.0 and LockBit 3.0 (also known as LockBit Black) being the most notable versions, each introducing new features and increasing the ransomware's effectiveness. LockBit operations are characterized by their speed, sophistication, and the use of a double extortion scheme.

LockBit attacks have been reported globally, affecting organizations in North America, Europe, Asia, and other regions, underscoring its operators' global ambitions and capabilities. It does not specifically target individual sectors but has been observed attacking organizations across healthcare, financial services, industrial, legal, and government sectors among others. The primary criterion appears to be the ability of the target to pay a substantial ransom.

LockBit uses a combination of symmetric (AES) and asymmetric (RSA) encryption algorithms. Files are encrypted with AES, while the AES key is encrypted with an RSA public key, ensuring that decryption is only possible with the corresponding private key held by the attackers. It automates the encryption process upon infection and can spread rapidly within a network, making it one of the fastest-spreading ransomwares. It targets a wide array of file types, excluding those necessary for the operating system to run, to avoid rendering the system completely inoperable.

LockBit commonly exploits vulnerabilities in exposed remote desktop services, VPNs, or other public-facing applications. Phishing campaigns and the use of previously compromised credentials are also frequent vectors for gaining initial access. Once inside the network, LockBit operators often use legitimate administrative tools and scripts to perform reconnaissance, move laterally, and escalate privileges. This technique, known as "living off the land", makes detection more challenging.

Table 3.1 shows the techniques and the tactics according to the MITRE ATT&CK framework, used by LockBit to compromise and exploit targeted networks[1]. We mainly

---

[1]https://www.cisa.gov/news-events/cybersecurity-advisories/aa23-165a

TABLE 3.1
LockBit Affiliates' MITRE ATT&CK Techniques.

Tactic	Technique ID	Technique Description
Initial Access	T1189	Drive-by Compromise
Initial Access	T1190	Exploit Public-Facing Application
Initial Access	T1133	External Remote Services
Initial Access	T1566	Phishing
Initial Access	T1078	Valid Accounts
Execution	T1059.003	Command and Scripting Interpreter: Windows Command Shell
Execution	T1072	Software Deployment Tools
Execution	T1569.002	System Services: Service Execution
Persistence	T1547	Boot or Logon Autostart Execution
Persistence	T1078	Valid Accounts
Privilege Escalation	T1548	Abuse Elevation Control Mechanism
Privilege Escalation	T1547	Boot or Logon Autostart Execution
Privilege Escalation	T1484.001	Domain Policy Modification: Group Policy Modification
Privilege Escalation	T1078	Valid Accounts
Defense Evasion	T1480.001	Execution Guardrails: Environmental Keying
Defense Evasion	T1562.001	Impair Defenses: Disable or Modify Tools
Defense Evasion	T1070.001, T1070.004	Indicator Removal: clears the Windows Event Logs files and deletes itself from the disk
Defense Evasion	T1027, T1027.002	Obfuscated Files or Information
Credential Access	T1110	Brute Force
Credential Access	T1555.003	Credentials from Password Stores: Credentials from Web Browsers
Credential Access	T1003, T1003.001	OS Credential Dumping including LAAS memory
Discovery	T1046	Network Service Discovery
Discovery	T1082	System Information Discovery
Discovery	T1614.001	System Location Discovery: System Language Discovery
Lateral Movement	T1021.001, T1021.002	Remote Services: Remote Desktop Protocol and Server Message Block (SMB)/Admin Windows Shares
Collection	T1560.001	Archive Collected Data: Archive via Utility
Command and Control	T1071.002, T1071.001	Application Layer Protocol: File Transfer Protocols and Web Protocols
Command and Control	T1095	Non-Application Layer Protocol
Command and Control	T1572	Protocol Tunneling
Command and Control	T1219	Remote Access Software
Exfiltration	T1567, T1567.002	Exfiltration Over Web Service and to Cloud Storage
Impact	T1485	Data Destruction
Impact	T1486	Data Encrypted for Impact
Impact	T1491.001	Defacement: Internal Defacement
Impact	T1490	Inhibit System Recovery
Impact	T1489	Service Stop

observe that Lockbit and its affiliates use a broad array of tactics and techniques from the MITRE ATT&CK framework underscores the sophistication of their operations. LockBit employs a wide range of initial access vectors, from exploiting public-facing applications and remote services to phishing and the use of valid accounts. This diversity in attack vectors demonstrates LockBit's adaptability and the broad spectrum of tactics it uses to gain entry into targeted systems. Once access is gained, LockBit affiliates execute malicious commands using batch scripts and Windows command shells, and deploy software tools to maintain their presence. This indicates a strategic approach to ensure continued access to the compromised system for further malicious activities. The table highlights techniques aimed at escalating privileges and evading defenses, including abusing elevation control mechanisms and impairing defense tools. This suggests LockBit's focus on gaining extensive control over compromised systems while minimizing detection by security tools. Techniques for accessing credentials and discovering network services are critical for LockBit's operations, allowing for lateral movement within networks and access to sensitive information. Before exfiltrating data, Lockbit uses tools like 7-zip to compress and encrypt data. The command and control communications are realized by employing application layer protocols including File Transfer Protocols (FTP) and Web Protocols for enabling discreet communication with compromised systems. It uses also Non-Application Layer Protocols by using tools like Ligolo for establishing SOCKS5 or TCP tunnels from a reverse connection, allowing the attackers to bypass network defenses and maintain stealthy control over the compromised systems. Protocol Tunneling and Remote Access Software techniques are also employed by LockBit with tools like Plink for SSH actions and leverages remote access software (e.g., AnyDesk, Atera RMM) for direct control over the victim's network, further facilitating lateral movement and data access. LockBit utilizes its custom tool, StealBit, for data theft, alongside publicly available file-sharing services and cloud storage management tools like Rclone and FreeFileSync. This enables the comprehensive and systematic removal of data from the target network, setting the stage for the double extortion scheme. The data exfiltration is done over publicly accessible web services, including cloud storage, which helps in anonymizing the attackers' activities and complicating traceability.

Lockbit and affiliates have a large impact vectors. They can delete log files, empty recycle bins, and encrypt data across Windows, Linux devices, and VMware instances to disrupt availability to system and network resources significantly. The malware changes the system's wallpaper to the LockBit wallpaper as a form of defacement and deletes volume shadow copies to inhibit system recovery efforts. It terminates essential processes and services to cripple the victim's operations further, ensuring that recovery is as difficult and time-consuming as possible.

LockBit is designed to quickly encrypt files across a network with minimal detection, often completing its encryption routine before effective countermeasures can be deployed. Starting with LockBit 2.0, the group adopted the double extortion tactic, where data is not only encrypted but also exfiltrated. Victims are then threatened with the public release of their data on the LockBit leak site if the ransom is not paid. It also introduced a feature that allows the ransomware to spread itself across network shares and removable drives, further automating the attack process.

LockBit operates on an affiliate model, where developers recruit affiliates to deploy the ransomware. Profits from ransom payments are split between the developers and the affiliates, incentivizing widespread distribution. LockBit represents a significant threat to organizations worldwide due to its aggressive encryption tactics, sophisticated exploitation of vulnerabilities, and the psychological pressure exerted by its double extortion scheme.

Ransomware evolution

Through the analysis of four major ransomware and early attempts, we mainly observe their evolution over years regarding their attack operations and the increasing level of sophistication. Table 3.2 shows the progression from relatively straightforward ransom demands based on opportunistic infections (CryptoLocker) to more sophisticated, targeted attacks that exploit specific vulnerabilities and use advanced tactics like worm-like propagation, manual operations, and double extortion (WannaCry, Ryuk, and LockBit). The evolution reflects not only advancements in the technical sophistication of ransomware but also in the strategic approach to choosing targets and maximizing profits.

TABLE 3.2

Comparative Analysis of CryptoLocker, WannaCry, Ryuk, and LockBit Ransomware

Feature	CryptoLocker	WannaCry	Ryuk	LockBit
Scope	Global, targeted	Global, indiscriminate	Selective, high-value organizations	Global, indiscriminate but focuses on lucrative targets
Targets	Individual users, small businesses	Organizations, healthcare, government, various sectors	Large enterprises, critical infrastructure	Various industries, focus on entities able to pay substantial ransoms
Encryption	AES and RSA encryption, files renamed with ".lockbit"	Uses AES and RSA, worm capabilities, ".WCRY" extension	Uses AES and RSA, targets specific critical files	Uses AES and RSA, known for fast and automated encryption process
Attack Vectors	Phishing emails, malicious attachments	SMB vulnerability (EternalBlue), spread autonomously	Spear-phishing, RDP vulnerabilities, follows infections like Emotet or TrickBot	Exposed remote services, VPNs, phishing, compromised credentials
Attack operations	Encrypted files and demanded ransom	Worm-like propagation, demanded ransom in Bitcoin, kill switch	Manual operation, data exfiltration, high ransom demands	Automated spreading, double extortion, "living off the land"

3.2 Building a Representative Ransomware Corpus

In a 1998 study Pearson [66] accurately enumerates a set of parameters marking the criteria to be compliant with in the compilation of a source corpus. In detail, the specifications of a corpus should respect the following:

- Time: the source corpus should be constituted of updated documentation in order to capture the knowledge shared in a specific domain. The conceptual framework should reflect the ongoing informative spectrum and, therefore, represent the fields of study in a streamlined context;

- Space: Documents present in a source corpus should not only adhere to updated information to represent a domain under investigation, but also refers to a specific spatial area. The observation of certain geographic contexts can support the identification of the main elements debated in given areas and meant to be covered by collecting the documentation;

- Language: A source corpus should contain documents written in the same language to guarantee a level of uniformity in the expression of knowledge through the conceptual framework;

- Authoritativeness: Documents in a source corpus should be published by different experts referring to a specific field of study in order to ensure the preciseness and suitability of information structuring;

- Formal integrity: In a source corpus another aspect to take into account involves the integrity of documents, meaning the exclusion of fragmented textual contents which could hinder the completeness of the data. By saying that, documents should respect the integrity principle also means keeping the originality of texts to be collected.

A corpus is a collection of "pieces of language that are selected and ordered according to explicit linguistic criteria in order to be used as a sample of the language" (Eagles 1996 [1]). The number of documents a corpus is supposed to gather is not a predetermined quantity, still in the literature the studies across the Corpus Linguistics framework emphasize the importance of collecting a sizeable set of data that can cover the knowledge proper to specific fields of interest in order to obtain a high level of representativeness in terms of the information correctly included to understand the domain under study (in this regard, the works published by Leech 1991;1992 [50][77], Biber 1993 [38], Pastor and Seghiri 2010 [49], Trunfio et al. 2014[3], Gray 2017 [16], Kaguera 2018 [106] represent some of the main scientific contributions in the literature).

Since a corpus is a sampling of a particular language or sublanguage, which contains an infinite amount of data, it must be representative and balanced if it claims to faithfully represent the facts in that language or sublanguage.

John Sinclair. 1987 [119]
Looking Up —An account of the COBUILD Project in Lexical Computing.

The threshold size of a corpus to be representative with respect to a specialized type of domain can be measured according to several strategies. One of the approaches, according to Hunston (2002) [114], is to create a solid basis of documents that are updated in accordance with the period of study. Therefore, the coverage of a corpus is computed through the consideration of the compliance with the variability of language within it and the capability of the documentation to cope with these linguistic structures. The novelty in the language characterizing the documents of a corpus can be also retrieved by the topics they are related to. Consequently, another strategy that can be envisaged for the maintenance of a suitable level of coverage is the identification of as many topics and sub-topics as possible in a documentation relating to an area of study (Clifton 1999). The level of information richness, following the reflections within the Lancaster University section for studying corpora[2], can be achieved by putting together a heterogeneous group of texts, i.e., documents which refer to several genres, whether they are *generalized* or *specialized* documentation referring to diverse levels of materials to analyze to represent a domain under investigation. Once multiple typologies of textual information collection have been created, the saturation point may be reached if there is a terminological dimension covering the whole variability of lexicon. Alongside the importance given by Corpus Linguistics to the adaptability of a collection of documents to the language variability and the diversity in genres, in the literature a set of studies has addressed the issue of corpus representativeness from a statistical perspective, such as those of Pastori and Seghiri or Trunfio et al. The aim of these works has specifically targeted the attempt of providing a measurement to calculate the minimum size for corpora to be considered representative of a specific knowledge framework by taking into account the term density balanced with the number of documents as well as the technicality in the information represented.

3.2.1 Specialized source corpus features

In this work the implementation of the semantic annotation model has been trained over a source corpus made up of the detected information within the list of CVE descriptions. In detail, the corpus has been created mapping a sample of CVE descriptions with known ransomware which have been detected starting by taking into account specialized security reports from 2007 up to 2023. The ransomware has been linked to the corresponding vulnerability descriptions by taking into account authoritative sources of information, such as the Cyber Security organization reports and reports from the Community Emergency Response Team (CERT) [3], the European Union Agency for Cybersecurity (ENISA) [4], the Agence nationale de la sécurité des systèmes d'informationANSSI (ANSSI) [5], the Cybersecurity and Infrastructure Security Agency (CISA) [6]. The training set construction which has been used to start the semantic annotation procedure over the CVE descriptions, has been organized by taking into account a grouping subdivision with a time-based criterion. Table 3.3 shows the whole labeled dataset from which we started our analysis to create an automatic code to extract knowledge and the descriptions selected for the development of a training set by considering the average proportion.

The textual structure of the descriptions follows the JSON formatting rules. The objective is to set a group of fixed expressions to be retrieved within all the descriptions of vulnerabilities associated with precise ransomware and annotate them as to build a ransomware knowledge base. In order to correctly proceed with the annotation, the texts have been pre-processed deleting the metadata elements and leaving the textual content meant to be analyzed.

---

[2]http://corpora.lancs.ac.uk/clmtp/answers.php?chapter=1&type=questions,Accessed15/04/2024
[3]https://community.fema.gov/PreparednessCommunity/s/welcome-to-cert?language=en_US
[4]https://www.enisa.europa.eu/
[5]https://www.ssi.gouv.fr/
[6]https://www.cisa.gov/

TABLE 3.3

Details of ransomware dataset.

Year	N. of Ransomware	N. of CVEs	Ransomware status	Training set
2007	**1**	**2**	**oldest**	**Yes**
2008	2	9	oldest	No
2009	0	0	oldest	No
2010	**13**	**383**	**oldest**	**Yes**
2011	0	0	oldest	No
2012	**6**	**97**	**oldest**	**Yes**
2013	16	169	oldest	No
2014	4	63	oldest	No
2015	**9**	**120**	**old**	**Yes**
2016	9	108	old	No
2017	**18**	**105**	**old**	**Yes**
2018	13	80	old	No
2019	**28**	**62**	**old**	**Yes**
2020	9	36	current	No
2021	**25**	**98**	**current**	**Yes**
2022	16	88	current	No
2023	**5**	**9**	**new**	**Yes**
Total	161	1410		

3.3   Ransomware CVE and ATT&CK Mappings Dataset

The dataset used to build our classification system of ransomware underpins our new approach to systematically understanding the behavior of ransomare threats regarding their exploited CVE and the associated MITRE ATT&CK techniques and tactics. With the help of cyber security experts, we built this dataset in a bottom-up fashion, linking each ransomware through specific citations in the literature to its CVE and the attack tactics and techniques. We also relied on Machine Learning techniques to build a classification system of CVE exploited by ransomware to their ATT&cK techniques and tactics.

3.3.1   Mapping of ransomware to their exploited CVE

The dataset has been built manually by taking into account the reliability of the sources [51], in our specific case those spreading information about the ransomware activities. In detail, the corpus has been compiled by checking security reports and news publicly available on the main cybersecurity portals, such as the CERT, ENISA or ANSSI. The different security and cyber threat intelligence-related information sources we consulted are represented in Table 3.4.

CVEs associated with each ransomware by using multiple sources have been validated by domain experts in the field of cybersecurity in order to verify the reliability of the mapped data. Our dataset contains a total number of **161 ransomware** which have been detected in a time-span going from **2007 to 2023**.

3.3.2   Mapping of ransomware to their ATT&CK tactics and techniques

We mapped each CVE exploited by a ransomware with its associated MITRE ATT&CK tactics and techniques. This task has been executed manually by searching and cross-checking

TABLE 3.4

Data sources used for building mappings between ransomware and their exploited CVE.

Type	Data sources
Cyber Security organisation reports	Reports from CERT, ENISA, ANSSI, CISA, etc.
Cyber security forums	KrebsOnSecurity, BleepingComputer, etc.
Specialized cyber security web sites	Threatpost, DarkReading, Hackread, TheHackerNews
Cyber security bulletins	Security alert reports by software and hardware providers
Reports from cyber security companies	Symantec, MacAfee, Kaspersky Lab, et CrowdStrike
Community forums on cyber security	Reddit: */r/netsec, /r/ransomware*

multiple data sources. In particular, we mainly relied on the reliable CISA and FBI alerts[7] for direct mapping between well-known ransomware and their used tactics and techniques. In addition, for the mapping between CVE and ATT&CK, we used and cross-checked multiple public datasets.

We first used a mapping of CVE to ATT&CK through its associated CAPEC information that is linked to CWE. These relations CVE ⟷ CWE ⟷ CAPEC ⟷ ATT&CK allowed us to have a mapping of 21196 CVE with 45 techniques. Secondly, we scraped and collected other public datasets and reports that contain multiple mappings between CVE and ATT&CK. The list of these data sources is shown in Table 3.5. We cross-checked these data sources and we mainly kept the mappings that are at least common to two of them. Our final dataset contains 8369 mappings that served as a training set for Machine Learning (ML) classification models.

TABLE 3.5

Data sources used for mapping CVE to ATT&CK techniques.

Dataset	CVEs	Techniques	Data source
MITRE relationships	21196	45	
Ackcent T1189	52	1	
AlienVault OTX	187	248	`https://otx.alienvault.com/`
AttackerKB	53	51	`https://attackerkb.com/`
Enisa Vuln-report	8 077	51	`https://github.com/enisaeu/vuln-report`
Helk	19	11	
Misc	5	6	
MITRE mapping	71	51	
rcATT	241	174	`https://github.com/vlegoy/rcATT`
Sigma	31	21	
TDM SocPrime	105	35	`https://tdm.socprime.com/`
Tram	25	7	`https://github.com/mitre-attack/tram`
Total	25 564	327	

We evaluated some well-established supervised ML algorithms to classify the CVE exploited by ransomware to their respective ATT&CK techniques and tactics. The ML classifier takes as input the textual description of a CVE and provides as output the list of associated techniques. We mainly evaluated three ML algorithms for this classification task:

---

[7]https://www.cisa.gov/stopransomware/alerts

- FastText[8]: a library developed by Facebook's AI Research (FAIR) team for efficient learning of word representations and sentence classification. It extends the ideas of word embeddings such as Word2Vec, but differs in significant ways that allow it to achieve high performance and accuracy for a wide variety of NLP tasks. Unlike traditional word embeddings like Word2Vec, which treats each word as a distinct entity, FastText uses subword information by breaking words into a set of n-grams (a contiguous sequence of n items from a given sample of text). FastText combines these character n-grams into a single word vector. It assigns a vector to each n-gram and the word vector is computed as the sum of these n-gram vectors. This approach allows the embeddings to share representations across word morphologies, improving performance on rare words or words not seen during training. In addition to word representation, FastText is also designed for text classification. It uses the bag of tricks (BoT) model where the average of the word vectors in a document is used to predict the label of the document.

- NBSVM[9]: a hybrid machine learning algorithm that combines the probabilistic framework of Naive Bayes (NB) with the linear classification of Support Vector Machines (SVM). This approach was proposed by Wang and Manning [130] to enhance the performance of text classification tasks by leveraging the strengths of both models. NBSVM modifies the input features by using a combination of the term frequency and the Naive Bayes log-count ratios. For each feature (word), the algorithm calculates the ratio of probabilities under each class. These ratios are then used to transform the frequency counts from the original data into weighted versions, emphasizing words that are more discriminative for the classes. It uses these transformed features to train a linear SVM classifier. The rationale is that these new features help in reducing the noise and emphasizing words that have strong predictive power due to their likelihood ratios.

- Bidirectional GRU (BIGRU): an advanced variant of the basic recurrent neural networks (RNNs) designed to improve the modeling of sequence data by processing it in both forward and backward directions. This bidirectional approach is particularly beneficial in the context of text classification, where understanding the context from both previous and subsequent words can provide a more comprehensive understanding of the text's overall meaning. In text classification, BiGRUs can capture nuances in language that might be missed when text is read only in the original order. For example, the importance of a word in a sentence can depend significantly on words that follow it, which standard unidirectional RNNs would miss.

TABLE 3.6

Performance of the three classification algorithms of CVE to ATT&CK techniques.

Algorithm	Accuracy	Precision	Recall	F1-score
FastText	0.62	0.84	0.73	0.78
BIGRU	0.66	0.86	0.74	0.80
NBSVM	0.67	0.83	0.74	0.78

We use the library Ktrain[10] for the implementation of these algorithms and evaluate their performance regarding the classification of CVE descriptions according to their ATT&CK techniques. Before training the models and for each CVE, we made a pre-processing of its

---

[8]https://fasttext.cc/
[9]https://github.com/mesnilgr/nbsvm
[10]https://github.com/amaiya/ktrain/

textual description by removing stop words, special characters, tabulations, and new lines. We also applied a lemmatization process by grouping together words to their root forms so they are analyzed as a single item, therefore as an example "escalation", "escalated", "escalating" will be replaced by "escalate".

The performance results according to the accuracy, precision, recall, and F1-score metrics of the three classifiers are depicted in Table 3.6. We have observed that the BIGRU provided better performance than the other two, and we used this algorithm classifying ransomware CVE to their respective attack techniques. Then, by understanding each technique associated to a given CVE, we used the ATT&CK matrix to identify its respective tactic.

4

Semantic Modeling and Knowledge Classification

In this chapter the methodology pursued for the purposes of achieving a classification scheme to structure to systematize the knowledge on ransomware retrieved by the semantic annotation procedure from CVE descriptions will be presented. In particular, the first part of the section will address the description of the semantic annotation procedure carried out over the texts included in the CVE list in order to train a model which can automatically detect the salient information to isolate and select to be integrated in the classification tool. The primary elements of this chapter will focus on the identification of the main representative concepts within the source corpus made up of CVE textual descriptions, then on the formalization of this knowledge through a pattern-based approach aimed at detecting a semantic recursive chain to be formalized in the classification scheme, which in this research will be represented by means of an ontological framework. The latter point will be addressed structuring the hierarchical configuration through main classes considered as entry points for the ontology system. The second part of this section will cover the identification of regular expressions within CVE. The third part of the section will show the connection between the vulnerabilities described in the CVE and the ransomware within the classification tool, as well as the statistic and semantic analysis.

4.1   Semantic Annotation of Source Corpus Documents

The corpus from which the methodological phase has taken its ground is constituted by the textual descriptions gathered from the CVE platform, published by the MITRE organism, mentioned in Chapter 3.

> When a vulnerability is initially discovered, the Common Enumeration Vulnerability (CVE) is usually the first structured source to ingest the new information and it provides, most importantly, a unique identification number (CVE-ID), as well as a few sentence overview.
>
> Bridges et al. 2013 [27]
> Automatic Labeling for Entity Extraction in Cyber Security

The period of reference considered to develop the source corpus equals to 16 years, going from 2007 to 2023 and overall the amount of the descriptions is 1410 associated with 161

DOI: 10.1201/9781003528999-4

known ransomware. The CVE descriptions are consistently presented in a structured format. As indicated in the CVE web platform[1], there are some measures to be compliant with when inserting a CVE record to define a discovered vulnerability. In detail, the minimum set of CVE record required includes:

- the name of the *affected Product* and the versions affected or fixed;

- the record ID for the CVE;

- the insertion of the *vulnerability type* or the *root cause* or the *impact*;

- one public reference at least;

- a *prose description*.

Name	Description
CVE-2019-5039	An exploitable command execution vulnerability exists in the ASN1 certificate writing functionality of Openweave-core version 4.0.2. A specially crafted weave certificate can trigger a heap-based buffer overflow, resulting in code execution. An attacker can craft a weave certificate to trigger this vulnerability.

FIGURE 4.1
Description of CVE-2010-5039.

Figure 4.1 shows the typical prose description published for a CVE included in the list provided by MITRE. For what concerns the last requirement, the CVE record is generally accompanied by a series of information, most of the time in English, useful to understand a certain vulnerability existing in given systems. In particular, the majority of the prose descriptions have a recursive construction of the sentences which allows the application of rules to retrieve meaningful information about the vulnerabilities. In this research the behavior of ransomware is analyzed through a cross-mapping of the attacks occurred in the infrastructures exploiting certain vulnerabilities, a data resulting from the connection of source corpus documentation and CVE. In the following subsections the formalization of the concepts related to the ransomware behavior from a semantic perspective starting from the CVE prose definitions will be thoroughly described.

4.1.1 Identification of representative concepts

In order to run a semantic systematization over the knowledge associated with ransomware exploitation of vulnerabilities, the first step to be addressed has been represented by the identification of the main concepts within the CVE textual lines to be organized in the taxonomic system. The combination of the CVE descriptions with a set of known ransomware allowed the systematization of a correspondence matrix showing the typical behavior adopted by ransomware exploiting certain vulnerabilities to damage the infrastructures, as explained in the next section. In detail, the compiled source corpus has enabled a conceptual analysis which has been based on the assumption that there is a conceptual organization of information in a standardized way, namely a vulnerability is exploited by malicious software, in this case a ransomware, and the way it is exploited follows the criterion by which:

1. a *cause* is set as initial parameter since it is the source from which the attack can be executed taking advantage of certain vulnerabilities;

2. the attack is performed according to a determined *likelihood*;

---

[1]https://www.cve.org/About/Process

3. an actor is involved as the user performing the attack, therefore the *condition* by which the cyber attack is realized;

4. the informative systems go through the attack and this event provokes a series of *impacts*;

5. the attack is performed by carrying out specific *actions*;

6. the *effects* follow the actions accomplished by the attackers which occurred within the infrastructures.

Given these premises, the semantic analysis of the source corpus revealed six main concepts.: *cause, likelihood, condition, impact, action*, and *effect*. In the perspective of creating a classification tool to group the features proper to the ransomware behavior in a predictive broad view, the concepts isolated as the most representative in the CVE definitions have been detailed with key patterns to train a model in order to allow the automatic identification of these latter to be added in the ontological configuration as sub-classes. In particular, for each of the key high-level concepts a set of regular expressions has been designated as follows:

- for the concept of *cause*: "Unspecified vulnerability"; "not properly validate pointers during HTML object rendering"; "Use-after-free vulnerability"; "Double free vulnerability"; "Buffer overflow"; "Heap-based buffer overflow"; "Integer overflow"; "not properly validate pointers during access to Silverlight elements"; "Integer underflow"; "not properly restrict discovery of memory addresses"; "not properly process request handles"; "Stack-based buffer overflow"; "exploitable command execution"; "specially crafted weave certificate"; "injection vulnerability;" "Improper limitation of path names"; "not protect from uncontrolled recursion from self-referential lookups"; "mishandles negative offsets during decoding";

- for the concept of *likelihood*: "allow"; "can lead to", "may allow"; "can"; "has the ability to"; "could allow"; "may happen"; "might allow";

- for the concept of *condition*: "remote attackers"; "unauthenticated users"; "local users"; "unauthenticated users"; "user-assisted remote attackers"; "malicous actor"; "attacker"

- for the concept of *impact*:, "code execution", "denial of service" or "obtain privilege rights"; "affect confidentiality, integrity, and availability"; "execute arbitrary code"; "execute arbitrary JavaScript code"; "conduct cross-site scripting (XSS) attacks"; "affect integrity"; "unspecified other impact"; "determine the existence of local pathnames, UNC share pathnames, intranet hostnames, and intranet IP addresses"; "gain privileges"; "obtain sensitive information"; "bypass the ASLR protection mechanism on Windows"; "unspecified impact on other platforms"; "read or write to arbitrary files"; "gain read-only access to unauthorized resources"; "Code Execution"; "gain unauthorized access"; "complete the authentication process"; "access an arbitrary file on the system"; "execute privileged commands"; "execute an arbitrary command on the system"; "Security Feature Bypass"; "Elevation of Priviledge"; "execute arbitrary code loaded from LDAP servers"; "execute arbitrary code on a Confluence Server or Data Center instance"; "download system files"; "Information Disclosure"; "access to internal API functions"; "information leak".

- for the concept of *action*:"crafted web site", "crafted tiff image", or "sending a handcrafted message"; "via a crafted (a) web site, (b) Office document, or (c) .rtf file"; "via crafted RTF data"; "via a crafted RTF document"; "Directory Traversal"; "via crafted SWF content"; "via unknown vectors related to Serviceability"; "via vectors involving crafted

JavaScript code, CMarkup, and the onpropertychange attribute of a script element"; "via vectors related to the CMarkup::IsConnectedToPrimaryMarkup function"; "via a crafted TrueType font"; "via an MP3 file with COMM tags that are mishandled during memory allocation"; "By using crafted input parameters"; "using System privileges"; "via a crafted EPS image"; "craft a weave certificate"; "via special crafted HTTP resource requests"; "authentication bypass"; "craft malicious input data"; "using a JNDI Lookup pattern"; "a crafted string is interpreted"; "upload arbitrary files through amavisd via a cpio loophole";

- for the concept of *effect*: "triggers access to a deleted object"; "overrides a valueOf function"; "leverages improper handling of the opaqueBackground property"; "triggers 'system state' corruption"; "trigger a heap-based buffer overflow"; "lead to incorrect access to any other user accounts".

4.1.2 Formalization of the retrieved knowledge from the source texts

Condamines (2008) [4] deals with the recurrent lexicon characterizing the level of linguistic variation within given specialized frameworks. Indeed, the retrieval process regarding the isolation of some fixed expressions, i.e., patterns, according to the author, results a simpler task when addressing fields of knowledge marked by a highly technical way of sharing textual information. The specificity proper to sector-oriented documentation enhances the identification of recurrent semantic structures because of the lexical fixity. The pattern-based configuration to be applied to specialized corpora can support the development of an entangled network of semantic relationships (Roesiger, 2016 [113]), which, in turn, can facilitate the automatic creation of knowledge organization systems, such as ontologies or thesauri (Lanza 2022 [36]). Barriére (2008) [2] offers an extended overview of some of the main existing works published on this subject addressing the patterns as supporting structures which interrelate two entities linked together by a semantic relation, as well as Musabeyezu (2019) [93] presenting a set of tools and techniques employed in the literature for annotation tasks. Meyer (2001) [65] states that these semantic recurrent chains are constituted by a "linguistic and paralinguistic elements that follow a certain syntactic order, and that permit to extract some conclusions about the meaning they express" (Meyer 2001:237). Barriére (2008) [2] provides a comprehensive definition of patterns, highlighting the connective structure they are characterized by to represent knowledge domain data.

In its most basic form, a pattern-based semantic relation would include a term X, a term Y, and a linguistic unit expressing a semantic relation between term X and Y. Finding instances of a semantic relation in texts using linguistic patterns can be implemented in different ways. It can be achieved by building a query where both X and Y are unknown terms linked by a known relation, as for example, is-a (X,Y). Another strategy can be applied to retrieve one unknown parameter and set the second parameter to a known value, for example the pattern is-a (X,drug).

Caroline Barrière et al. 2008
Pattern-based approaches to semantic relation extraction: A state-of-the-art

---

In the work of Lefeuvre (2017) [74] the relationships occurring between concepts related to given specialized fields of study are investigated under the lens of domain specificity.

The author specifically focuses on the patterns as lexical units recursive in specific texts which belong to the domain of interest. The relations taken into account by the author are the hierarchical ones, represented by terms in contexts related to specialized areas of study that are connected through a part-whole association. The link between terms within textual information has been extensively examined in the studies of Hearst [81] who provided a set of lexical batteries to identify the hyponymy structure in the texts, such as, Nounphrases followed by the adverbial construction "such as" and other Nounphrases. Corpus Pattern Analysis (CPA) has represented an investigation path for a wide range of works in the literature, such as Hanks (2014;2017) [102][61], Campos (2013) [30], El Maarouf(2013)[44], Araùz (2009) [12].

Corpus Pattern Analysis (CPA) assumption

CPA starts from the observation that whereas most words are very ambiguous, most patterns have one and only one sense. Each word is associated with a number of patterns based on valency, which is comparatively stable, and one or more sets of preferred collocations, which are highly variable (Hanks 2012). In CPA, patterns of word use are associated with statements of meaning, called implicatures. Each pattern has a primary implicature (the meaning of the pattern), and possibly a number of secondary implicatures (de Schryver 2010).

Hanks Patrick et al.2017
Flexibility of multiword expressions and Corpus Pattern Analysis

---

Following the considerations of Hanks, CPA represents a technique for "mapping meaning onto words in text"(2004:87), and each word unit meaning is connected to "prototypical contexts". The isolation of verbal patterns and noun patterns [86], a task characterizing the CPA, is strictly connected with the genre of texts under analysis. As underlined by Condamines (2011) [37], indeed, a strong level of dependency exists between the conceptual framework of a specialized field of knowledge and the patterns used to represent it. As a matter of fact, the author in 2002 [37] stressed the importance of determining the specificity of a source corpus.

First, a corpus is not simply a set of utterances in a language. It has been created with a precise objective and contains texts written by authors with a well-defined aim, at a precise time and for a particular set of readers. In brief, a corpus is linked together by significant extra-linguistic characteristics (named genre by Biber (Biber 1988)). Second, as a set of discursive realizations, a corpus appears in a linear form, as a set of linguistic elements entering into numerous and varied semantico-syntactic relations.

Anne Condamines. 2002
Corpus analysis and conceptual relation patterns

The author specifically addressed the issue that a pattern is a "distinctive element" in a conceptual context, which, being recurrent, simplifies a connection existing between entities of a domain, citing Pearson (1998) when saying that patterns are considered as "connective phrases", or Bowden et al. (2000) in interpreting them as "explicit relation marker". The study by Condamines explores the several ways in which these recurrent patterns can lead to a relational structure when analysing a corpus. However, the author particularly focuses on the relevance of genre in the texts constituting the corpus since it influences the selection of domain-oriented expression to retrieve a desired set of information. When constructing a path to schematize the patterns batteries, a verb is usually considered as the key component to take into account to set the connections in a phrase, but, as Condamines points out, there is a risk of lacking the preliminary knowledge about the domain-information structure: "Verb role is then fundamental since the associated role of any argument can be used to identify relations between two of them. This kind of pattern requires the construction of lists corresponding to semantic classes. For example, 'transmission predicates' or 'humans'. Such a requirement is problematic since it relies on semantic knowledge which is not necessarily stated in the corpus analyzed, and there is a risk that the semantic a priori knowledge does not correspond to real linguistic behavior in the corpus" (Condamines 2011:15). Hence, the advice is to consider not binary morphosyntactic relations, but instead a *n-ary scheme*.

Numerous studies in the literature provide a comprehensive understanding on the study of corpora through the examination of morphosyntactic recursive structures [127]. For instance, Hunston and Su (2019) [64] refer to grammar patterns and the groups of words to be used in order to create "candidate constructions". Contextual lexical relations have been analyzed by many authors in the phases of detecting salient information to be treated with NLP tasks. Storjohann (2005) [124] covers the issue of *sense relations* in the source corpora, stating that the "Instances of natural language are studied in order to identify rules and patterns, and linguistic proto-typicalities are then interpreted and classified" (Storjohann 2005:6). The author studies the typicalities within linguistic units as parts of a determined corpus from the perspective of a corpus-driven approach where a corpus is an "inventory of language data". From the corpus "appropriate material is extracted to support intuitive knowledge, to verify expectations, to allow linguistic phenomena to be quantified, and to find proof for existing theories or to retrieve illustrative samples. It is a method where the corpus is interrogated and data is used to confirm linguistic pre-set explanations and assumptions" (Storjohann 2005:8). Against this background, the author examines the information included within the inventory data from a collocation analysis approach where the principle of *contextual proximity* between terms in the sentences plays an important role in identifying the main kinds of patterns, i.e., "synonyms, hyperonyms, hyponyms, and in fewer cases, also terms of contrast and opposition". The concept of kinship in corpus modeling results to be fundamental to detect the most appropriate patterns through which a system of semantic annotation ([25]) can be efficient to provide a correct path towards the creation of the entities to be included in the classes of a taxonomic structure.

In the following sections the presentation of the class identification through rule-based patterns configuration will be provided, together with the description of the automatic identification of these latter through a Machine Learning task and the in-depth study of the ontology development starting from the *classes* identified and the features retrieved as *sub-classes* and *object properties* in the ontology structure.

4.1.2.1 Categories identification through pattern

The methodology of this research has relied on the assumption that CVE descriptions are characterized by a regular semantic chain in representing the main concepts related to the exploited vulnerabilities. In particular, as aforementioned, the starting element of the sentences of CVE prose descriptions is mostly represented by the *cause* determining a given *impact*, which is preceded by the *likelihood* and the *condition* through which a cause derives, then the second part of the descriptions deals with the *action* and the *effect* of the exploitation has on given infrastructures. The fixed sequence in which the terms are positioned in the sentences characterizing the CVE descriptions allows to train a rule-based pattern configuration aimed at identifying trigger morphosyntactic units. In the process of training a model to automatically detect the ransomware-associated information starting from CVE descriptions these patterns represent the key elements meant to be normalized in the corresponding *classes* and *subclasses* within the ontology framework, as well as useful parameters to create the semantic relations, i.e, object properties. The structure of the pattern configuration over CVE prose descriptions is depicted in Figure 4.2.

FIGURE 4.2
Patterns schema for categories annotation of CVE descriptions.

In particular, for each main category, a set of morphosyntactic rules has been defined. The following are some representative case of the rules applied:

- **CausePattern**: e.g., LEMMA (integer) + LEMMA (overflow) | ADJ (injection) + LEMMA (vulnerability) | VERB (infinitive: due) + PREP (to) + NOUN | ;LEMMA (double) + ADJ (free) + NOUN (vulnerability) | ADV (not) + ADV (e.g., properly) + VERB (process| validate| protect) + NOUN + NOUN;

- **LikelihoodPattern**: e.g., VERB (allow | may allow | can lead) + PREP (to) — NOUN (e.g., code) + NOUN (e.g., execution); VERB (allow | may allow | can lead) + **ConditionPattern configuration + the ImpactPattern configuration;**

- **ConditionPattern**: e.g., ADJ (remote | local) + NOUN (attacker); VERB (past participle: unauthenticated) + NOUN (e.g., users) + **ImpactPattern configuration**

- **ImpactPattern**: e.g., VERB (execute | perform) + ADJ (e.g., arbitrary) NOUN (e.g., code); LEMMA (denial) + PREP (of) NOUN (service); VERB (affect) + NOUN (confidentiality| integrity | availability); VERB (read | write) + PREP (to) + ADJ (e.g., arbitrary) + NOUN (e.g., files); NOUN (information) + NOUN (disclosure); NOUN (elevation) + PREP (of) + NOUN (privileges) + **ActionPattern configuration**

- **ActionPattern**: e.g., LEMMA (via) + PREP (a) + NOUN | + VERB (gerund: involving) + VERB (crafted) + NOUN (JavaScript) + NOUN; LEMMA (via) + VERB (past participle: unknown) + NOUN (vectors); VERB (upload) + ADJ (e.g., arbitrary) + NOUN (e.g.,files); LEMMA (via) + VERB (past participle: crafted) + NOUN (e.g., website | SWF | EPS | HTTP) + NOUN + **EffectPattern configuration**

- **EffectPattern**: e.g., PRON (that| which) + VERB (lead | leverage)+ PREP (to) + NOUN; VERB (trigger) + NOUN (e.g., access) + PREP + NOUN (e.g., system) + NOUN (e.g., state) + NOUN (e.g., corruption) — VERB (past participle, e.g., deleted) + NOUN (e.g., object)

Once having extracted a set of annotation sets to formalize the knowledge about ransomware starting from their exploitation of given vulnerabilities, a normalization process was defined. This task specifically supported the replacement of some of the retrieved expressions with the corresponding semantic equivalents when the first ones appeared to be repeated or not suitable for the noun-phrase construction, required in KOS structuring of terms representing concepts[2]. For instance, *arbitrary code execution* and *code execution* being semantically equivalent have been merged in one single unit: *code execution.*

To perform the normalization a transformer-based neural network computes similarities between each pairs of extracted features has been employed. To perform the semantic annotation procedure, the corpus has been analyzed through the use of a semantic tool Prodigy[3], a semantic annotator tool developed by Explosion, an expert software company in the construction of NLP tools, such as spaCy, and machine teaching implementation. The main functions granted by Prodigy refer to the semantic annotation of texts given in input, mostly in Json format, aimed at detecting the marking units in the textual data to train models towards automatic classification processes. The interface of Prodigy is based on a logic of snippets, i.e., the manual annotation is firstly based on a task related to the identification of the top categories which can be visualized in the main line of the box to annotate, and each time users can employ a snippet to highlight the portion of the text that is corresponding to the category under analysis (see Figure 4.3).

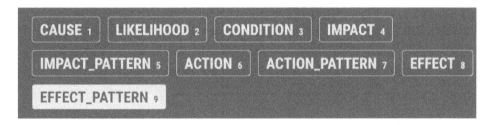

FIGURE 4.3
Main span of text categories annotated by using Prodigy.

The iteration Prodigy allows over the annotations represents a key method to improve the model training accuracy as well as the annotation efficiency. The process of semantic annotation started with the manual identification of the main concepts in the CVE descriptions formalized in the top-level main classes, then the use of Prodigy involved the following phases:

1. Creation of the subsets: separation of CVE descriptions in two sets, i.e., the training set constituted by 80% of texts and test set constituted by 20% of texts;

2. Model training: manual annotation for the training set;

3. Validation of the model: verification of the performance of the model trained during the second step;

4. Automatic annotation: execution of the pattern-based approach through the detection of trigger expressions learnt during the first steps to automatically retrieve the information over new texts in input of CVE prose descriptions.

---

[2]See ISO 25964-1:2011
[3]https://prodi.gy/

4.1.2.2 Spans categories annotation

Building a semantic model of CVE exploited by ransomware requires a dataset from which to start the manual annotation of their features defined as spans of text. To create the latter a group of CVE descriptions has been isolated as described in Chapter 3. Prodigy has been used to train a model to semantically associate the data to selected segments of the sentences. The tool provides an interface where the main classes (see Figure 4.3) are on the top of the box and users are able to highlight the portions of the text directly associated with the class chosen as representative of these ones. The Figures (from 4.4 to 4.13) show some of the examples of the training set using the semantic annotator tool which has constituted the starting point to allow the automatic identification of these patterns on new CVE descriptions during the next phase. Each set of annotations is characterized by the presence of the CVE ID and the associated name of the ransomware, the date deriving from the connective structure forged in the corpus compilation phase.

4.1.2.3 Spans categories model training and testing

The annotated CVE dataset with the 9 categories of spans of text as described in Figure 4.3 contains 240 unique CVEs of 95 ransomware. This dataset is used for training a model able to identify the same span categories in the large dataset of all the analyzed ransomware and their respective CVEs. The *spancat* model[4] is trained by using the Prodigy tool with its train recipe. The training phase is conducted on 192 samples and the evaluation phase with 48 samples (20%). The best trained model has an F1-score of 0.70, a Precision of 0.81 and a Recall of 0.62. For instance, by using the trained model, the following categories have been extracted from CVE-2013-2551 exploited by the BANDARCHOR ransomware:

- ACTION: crafted web site that triggers access to a deleted object
- CAUSE: Use-after-free vulnerability
- IMPACT: execute arbitrary code

The performance results of the trained model per span category is shown in Table 4.1. Simple constructed categories which are LIKELIHOOD and CONDITION have the best performance regarding the Precision, Recall, and F1-score. The two categories CAUSE and IMPACT that will be used to characterize the semantics of each CVE exploited by ransomware have also good evaluation performance. Then, the obtained model has been run using the Spacy library on the remaining set of CVEs to annotate all of them and extract their spans of texts categories.

TABLE 4.1
Performance metrics of the trained span categorizer per category type.

Span category	Precision	Recall	F1-score
LIKELIHOOD	83.87	74.29	78.79
CONDITION	89.47	79.07	83.95
CAUSE	92.31	52.17	66.67
IMPACT	81.40	68.63	74.47
IMPACT_PATTERN	80.95	56.67	66.67
ACTION	72.73	51.61	60.38
ACTION_PATTERN	70.00	53.85	60.87

[4]https://prodi.gy/docs/span-categorization

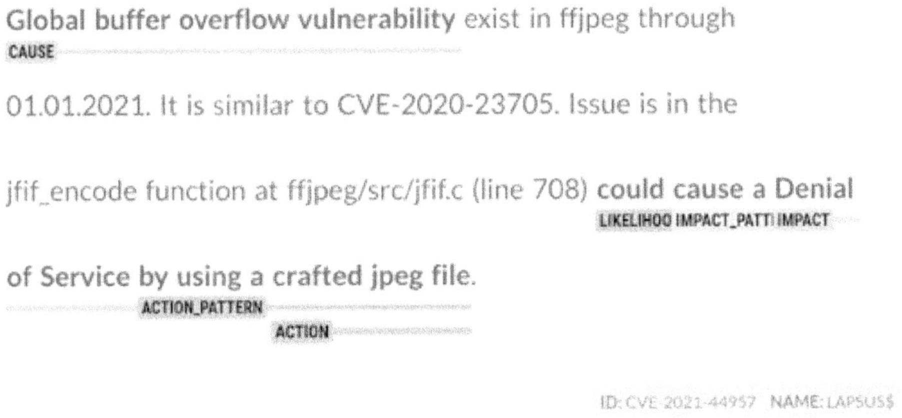

Global buffer overflow vulnerability exist in ffjpeg through
CAUSE

01.01.2021. It is similar to CVE-2020-23705. Issue is in the

jfif_encode function at ffjpeg/src/jfif.c (line 708) could cause a Denial
LIKELIHOO IMPACT_PATT IMPACT

of Service by using a crafted jpeg file.
ACTION_PATTERN
ACTION

ID: CVE-2021-44957 NAME: LAPSUS$

FIGURE 4.4
Annotation of CVE-2021-44957 of LAPSUS$ ransomware.

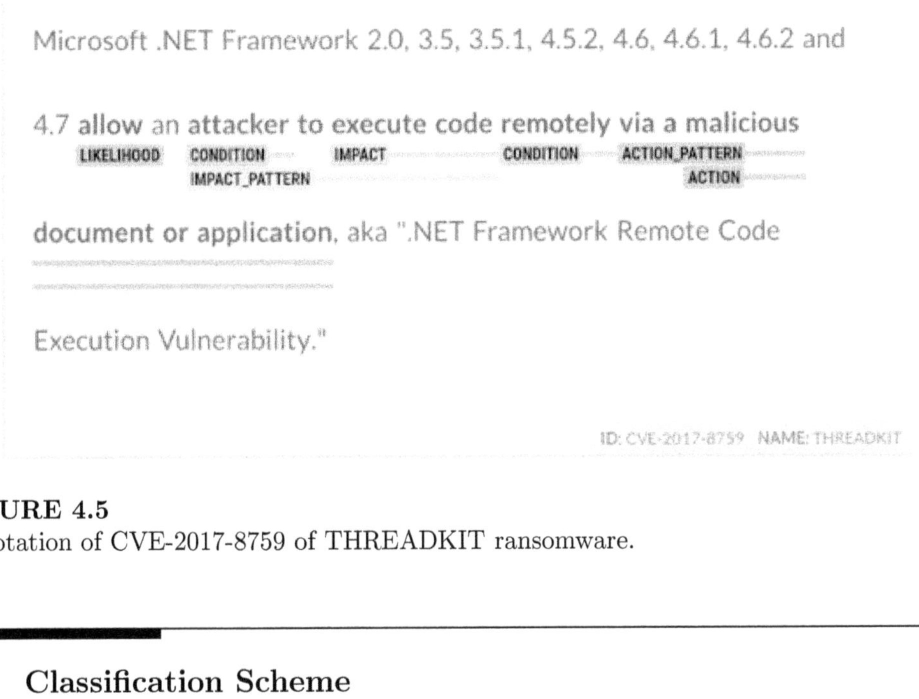

Microsoft .NET Framework 2.0, 3.5, 3.5.1, 4.5.2, 4.6, 4.6.1, 4.6.2 and

4.7 allow an attacker to execute code remotely via a malicious
LIKELIHOOD CONDITION   IMPACT   CONDITION   ACTION_PATTERN
            IMPACT_PATTERN   ACTION

document or application, aka ".NET Framework Remote Code

Execution Vulnerability."

ID: CVE-2017-8759 NAME: THREADKIT

FIGURE 4.5
Annotation of CVE-2017-8759 of THREADKIT ransomware.

4.2   Classification Scheme

On the basis of existing works in the literature mentioned in Chapter 2, this research has been oriented towards the development of a classification scheme by means of an ontological framework where the formalized knowledge within the CVE descriptions can be represented in a hierarchically structured way and with the use of relational properties. In detail, the object properties link together classes and also pairs of individuals, while data properties connect these latter with data values or literals[5]. The study carried out by More et al. (2012:76) [90] covers the creation of an ontology for the intrusion detection and prevention systems support.

---

[5]See W3C recommendations, https://www.w3.org/OWL/

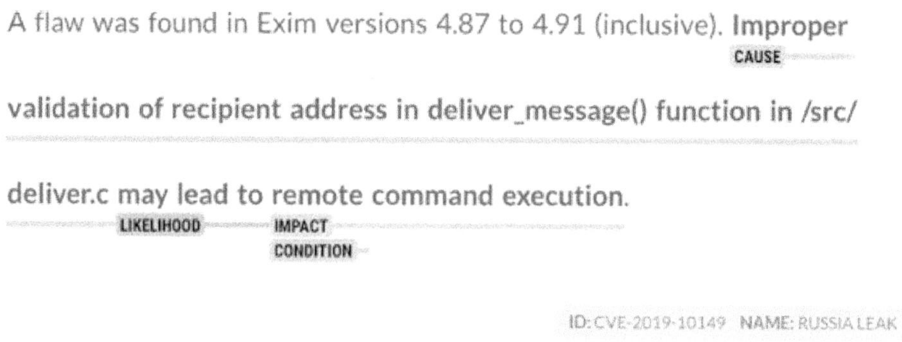

A flaw was found in Exim versions 4.87 to 4.91 (inclusive). **Improper**
                                                                 CAUSE

validation of recipient address in deliver_message() function in /src/

deliver.c may lead to remote command execution.
                    LIKELIHOOD   IMPACT
                                       CONDITION

ID: CVE-2019-10149   NAME: RUSSIA LEAK

FIGURE 4.6
Annotation of CVE-2019-10149 of RUSSIA LEAK ransomware.

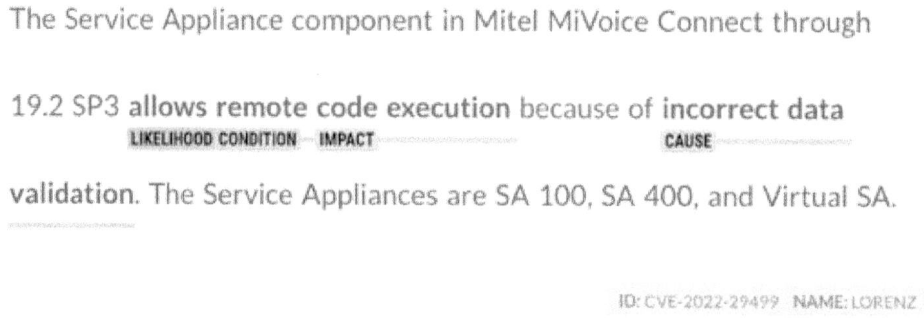

The Service Appliance component in Mitel MiVoice Connect through

19.2 SP3 **allows remote code execution** because of **incorrect data**
        LIKELIHOOD CONDITION   IMPACT   CAUSE

validation. The Service Appliances are SA 100, SA 400, and Virtual SA.

ID: CVE-2022-29499   NAME: LORENZ

FIGURE 4.7
Annotation of CVE-2022-29499 of LORENZ ransomware.

The ontology comprises of 3 fundamental classes: 'means', 'consequences', and 'targets'. The 'means' class encapsulates the ways and methods used to perform an attack, the 'consequences' class encapsulates the outcomes of the attack, and the 'target' class encapsulates the information of the system under attack. For instance, the 'means' class consists of sub-classes like 'BufferOverFlow', 'synFlood', 'LogicExploit', 'tcpPortScan', etc., which can further consist of their own sub-classes; the 'consequences' class consists of sub-classes like 'DenialOfService', 'LossOfConfiguration' 'PrivilegeEscalation', 'UnauthUser', etc.; and the 'targets' class consists of sub-classes like 'SystemUnderDoSAttack', 'SystemUnderProbe', 'SystemUnderSynFloodAttack', etc. The entities that are collected from different data streams are asserted into one of the classes based on the properties of the class and the meaning of the entity.

More et al. 2012
A Knowledge-Based Approach to Intrusion Detection Modeling

Another interesting reference study in line with this research is that proposed by Keshavarzi and Ghaffary in 2023 [70] on the ontology of digital blackmails, which they have

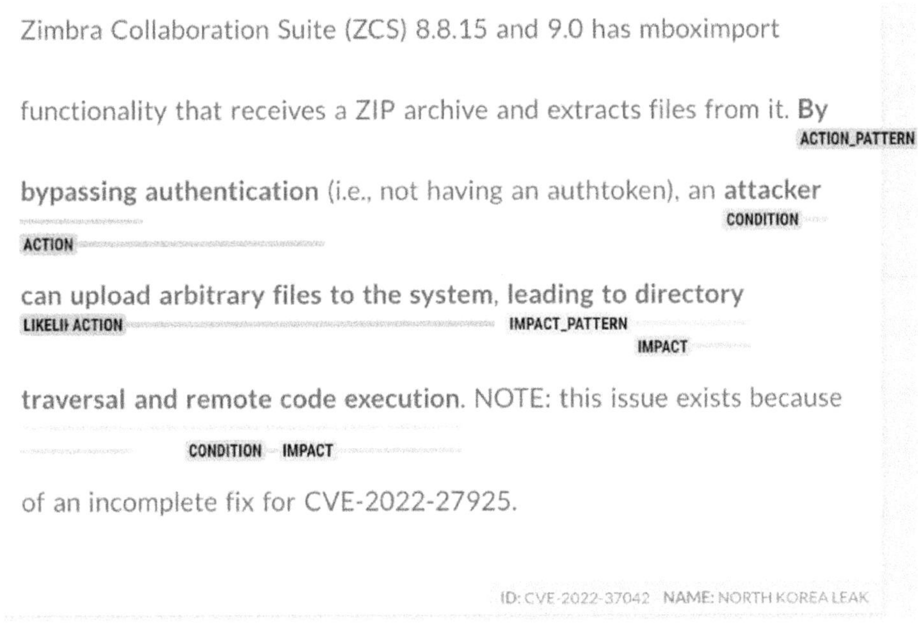

Zimbra Collaboration Suite (ZCS) 8.8.15 and 9.0 has mboximport

functionality that receives a ZIP archive and extracts files from it. **By**
ACTION_PATTERN

bypassing authentication (i.e., not having an authtoken), an **attacker**
CONDITION

ACTION

can upload arbitrary files to the system, leading to directory
LIKELIH ACTION   IMPACT_PATTERN
                                                                                        IMPACT

traversal and remote code execution. NOTE: this issue exists because

CONDITION   IMPACT

of an incomplete fix for CVE-2022-27925.

ID: CVE-2022-37042   NAME: NORTH KOREA LEAK

FIGURE 4.8
Annotation of CVE-2022-37042 of NORTH KOREA LEAK ransomware.

Zimbra Collaboration (aka ZCS) 8.8.15 and 9.0 has mboximport

functionality that receives a ZIP archive and extracts files from it. An

authenticated user with administrator rights has the ability to
CONDITION   LIKELIHOOD
                                                       ACTION_PATTERN

upload arbitrary files to the system, leading to directory traversal.
ACTION   IMPACT_PATTERN
                                            IMPACT

ID: CVE-2022-27925   NAME: NORTH KOREA LEAK

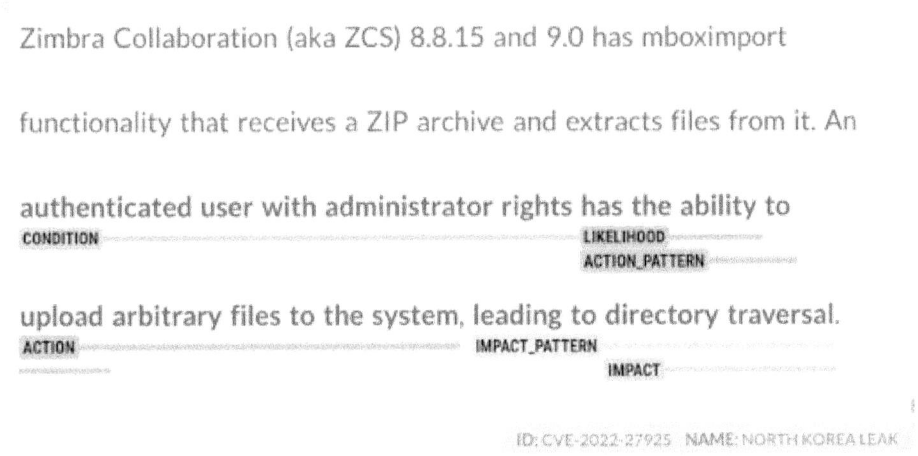

FIGURE 4.9
Annotation of CVE-2022-27925 of NORTH KOREA LEAK ransomware.

called *Rantology* "designed to explore the interactions of ransomware and benign software
with the system and to perceive the relationships between system API calls and the behaviors resulting from the execution of these binaries" (2023:4). The clarification given by the
authors is shared in the research presented in this monograph, that is the identification of
the ontology as the preferred tool to represent domain-dependent objects instead of a taxonomy, since the latter provides a limitation in just using a type of relation 'is-a'. The ontology,
on the other side, can ensure an exploration of the knowledge in a broader extensive way by
considering other forms of relations through the object properties and data properties. The

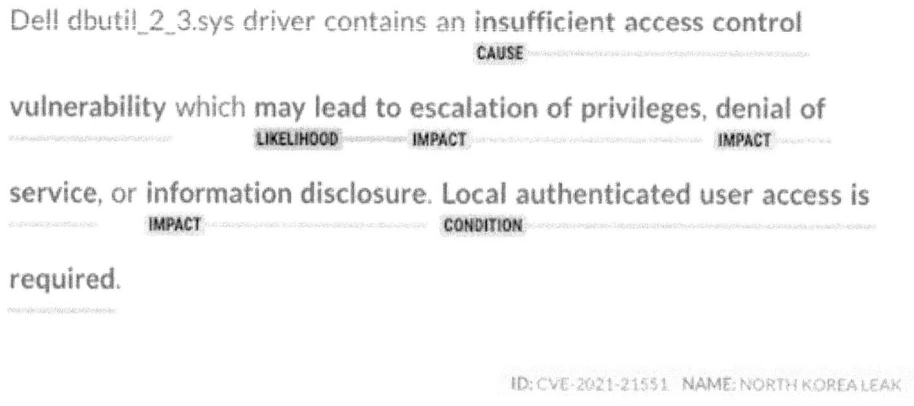

Dell dbutil_2_3.sys driver contains an **insufficient access control**
                                            CAUSE

vulnerability which **may lead to escalation of privileges, denial of**
                          LIKELIHOOD   IMPACT   IMPACT

service, or **information disclosure. Local authenticated user access is**
          IMPACT   CONDITION

required.

ID: CVE-2021-21551   NAME: NORTH KOREA LEAK

FIGURE 4.10
Annotation of CVE-2021-21551 of NORTH KOREA LEAK ransomware.

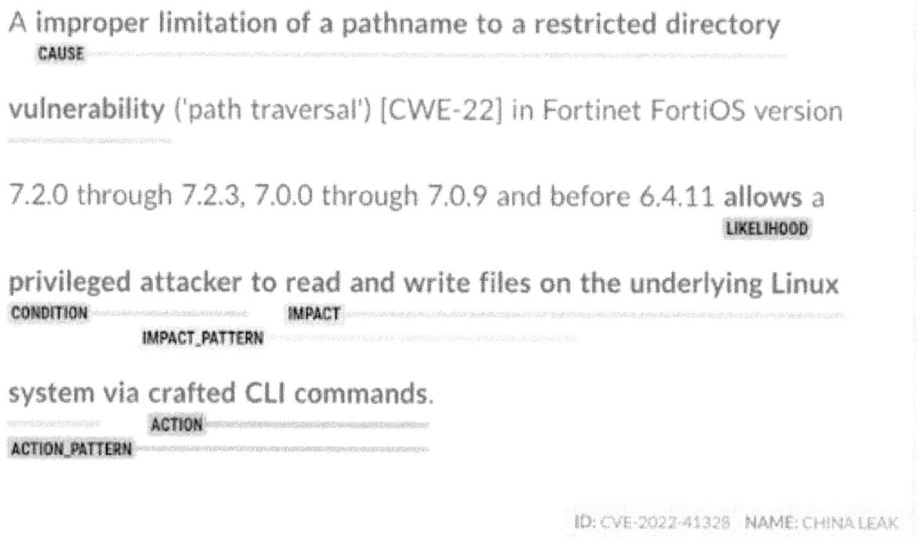

A **improper limitation of a pathname to a restricted directory**
  CAUSE

vulnerability ('path traversal') [CWE-22] in Fortinet FortiOS version

7.2.0 through 7.2.3, 7.0.0 through 7.0.9 and before 6.4.11 **allows** a
                                                            LIKELIHOOD

privileged attacker to read and write files on the underlying Linux
CONDITION   IMPACT
              IMPACT_PATTERN

system via crafted CLI commands.
                  ACTION
ACTION_PATTERN

ID: CVE-2022-41328   NAME: CHINA LEAK

FIGURE 4.11
Annotation of CVE-2022-41328 of CHINA LEAK ransomware.

authors specifically developed the ontology based on Windows ransomware which contains "all the entities associated with fear-based malware and digital blackmailers, various types of ransomware, system calls, ransom and payment methods, cyber threat actors, and other agents involved in this realm" (2023:4). Following the words of the authors "According to the concepts extracted in the scope of cyber extortion attacks and the application of this ontology, the terms *Software, Behavior, OperatingSystemAPI, PaymentSystem, CyberActor* and *ThreatComponent* are defined as the main classes. Core classes are located at the root level of the hierarchy, which are defined as subclasses of the most general class" (2023:6). By considering the principle of creating a system made up of classes and sub-classes as the aforementioned studies, the ontology hereby presented is built upon the four main classes detected during the annotation procedure (see Figure 4.14): *cause, condition, impact, action, effect* to which the subclasses associated are represented by the patterns retrieved

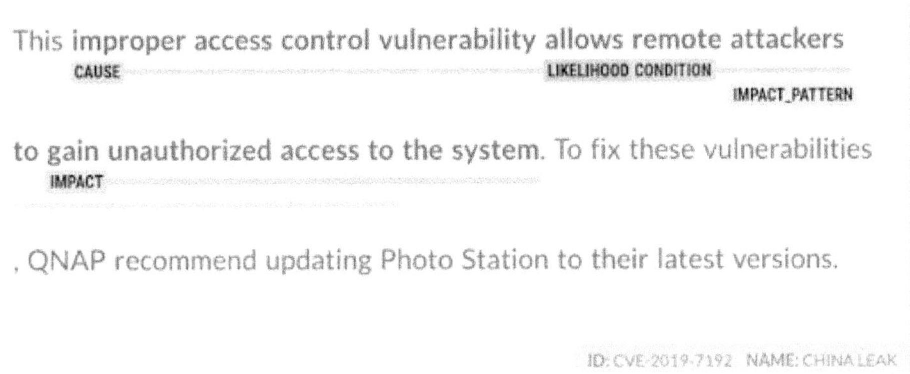
This improper access control vulnerability allows remote attackers
CAUSE
LIKELIHOOD CONDITION
IMPACT_PATTERN
to gain unauthorized access to the system. To fix these vulnerabilities
IMPACT
, QNAP recommend updating Photo Station to their latest versions.
ID: CVE-2019-7192 NAME: CHINA LEAK

FIGURE 4.12
Annotation of CVE-2019-7192 of CHINA LEAK ransomware.

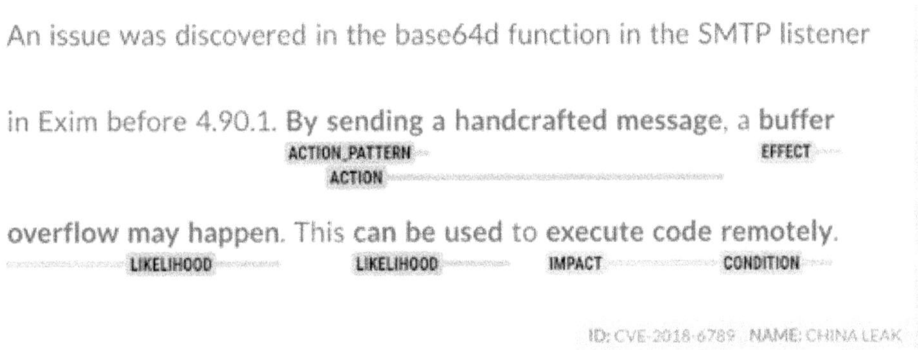
An issue was discovered in the base64d function in the SMTP listener
in Exim before 4.90.1. By sending a handcrafted message, a buffer
ACTION_PATTERN
EFFECT
ACTION
overflow may happen. This can be used to execute code remotely.
LIKELIHOOD
LIKELIHOOD
IMPACT
CONDITION
ID: CVE-2018-6789 NAME: CHINA LEAK

FIGURE 4.13
Annotation of CVE-2018-6789 of CHINA LEAK ransomware.

both in the model training phase and in the automatic phase on Prodigy. The *likelihood* is implemented as cardinality restriction which in OWL "allow us to say how many distinct values a property can have for any given subject" (Allemang and Hendler 2011 [10]).

owl:Thing
Tactic
Effect
Technique
Cause
Action
Impact
CVE
Ransomware

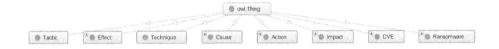

FIGURE 4.14
Ransomware ontology hierarchical structure.

4.2.1 Definition of knowledge representation levels

The semantically annotated corpus was then managed in high-level classes in the ontology system. The principle followed for the construction of the hierarchy is based on the **is-a** and **kindOf** relations formalization between classes and sub-classes and on the extension of object properties to further express the connections occurring among these groups of concepts of the semantic structure starting from the patterns identified in the training phase.

TABLE 4.2
Excerpt of CVE correspondence matrix
with related ransomware.

CVE ID	Ransomware
CVE-2010-0188	CRYPTOFORTRESS
CVE-2012-0507	CRYPTOFORTRESS
CVE-2012-0158	AKBUILDER
CVE-2012-1723	CRYPTOFORTRESS
CVE-2015-2419	PETYA
CVE-2015-3104	CRYPTOFORTRESS
CVE-2015-3113	PETYA
CVE-2015-5119	SEON
CVE-2017-0199	IRAN LEAK
CVE-2021-26855	LAPSUS$

For each CVE a specific ransomware has been identified according to the matrix of correspondences created during the corpus compilation phase, as depicted in a representative sample in Table 4.2. Each instance of vulnerability and ransomware has been considered in this research study as a sub-class in order to keep the same level of information distribution and granularity of information within the taxonomic configuration, as well as to guarantee a detailed overview of the connections they share with other classes of the ontology. In an ontological framework, indeed, the *individuals* correspond to the instances of a concept set as representative in a monodimensional way of an attribute specification, they are linked by *ObjectProperty*, and this would have lead, in a logic of keeping a homogeneous level of taxonomic subdivision preservation, to adjust the information included in the other classes as individuals, loosing in this way the gathering operations proper to classification. Sub-classes inherit the defined Object properties related to the classes to which they belong. Classes as *action* or *impact* contain several sub-classes correctly associated with this taxonomic level since they share certain features to be united as subdivision of higher classes and potentially expanded as including other instances. The ontology has been developed through the use of Protégé platform[6], which allows through its dynamic interface to manually complete the population of concepts belonging to specific domains of knowledge and their connective structure in specific tabs. The main classes are subdivided into sub-classes related to the concepts retrieved in the phase of pattern detection and then formalized to be part of a classification tool. For instance, the class *Impact* contains, in a normalized way of presenting the concepts within an ontological structure, 30 sub-classes, the class *Action* 27 sub-classes, the class *Ransomware* 96 sub-classes, the class *Effect* 5 sub-classes, the class *CVE* 152 subclasses, the class Technique 6 sub-classes, and the class Tactic 5 sub-classes. The last two classes will be expanded in the future works. The following list illustrates in alphabetical order the structure of the ontology with a few sub-classes of *CVE* and *Ransomware* to give a representation of how they have been positioned in the tree-structure. Per each entity, the list provides the type and the superclass connection:

Action: Class
Arbitrary files reading: Sub-Class (Action)
Authentication bypass: Sub-Class (Action)
Crafted .rtf file: Sub-Class (Action)
Crafted EPS image: Sub-Class (Action)

---

[6]https://protege.stanford.edu/

Crafted HTTP resource requests: Sub-Class (Action)
Crafted Office document: Sub-Class (Action)
Crafted RTF data: Sub-Class (Action)
Crafted RTF document: Sub-Class (Action)
Crafted SWF content: Sub-Class(Action)
Crafted TrueType font: Sub-Class (Action)
Crafted document: Sub-Class (Action)
Crafted input parameters: Sub-Class (Action)
Crafted malicious input data: Sub-Class (Action)
Crafted pathname in an executable file: Sub-Class (Action)
Crafted string: Sub-Class (Action)
Crafted tiff image: Sub-Class (Action)
Crafted weave certificate: Sub-Class (Action)
Crafted web site: Sub-Class (Action)
Directory Traversal vulnerability: Sub-Class (Action)
Handcrafted message: Sub-Class (Action)
JNDI Lookup pattern: Sub-Class (Action)
MP3 file with COMM tags: Sub-Class (Action)
System privileges: Sub-Class (Action)
Unknown vectors: Sub-Class (Action)
Unknown vectors related to Concurrency: Sub-Class (Action)
Unknown vectors related to Serviceability: Sub-Class (Action)
Vectors involving CMarkup: Sub-Class (Action)
Vectors involving crafted JavaScript code: Sub-Class (Action)

Cause: Class
Double free vulnerability: Sub-Class (Cause)
Heap-based buffer overflow: Sub-Class (Cause)
Improper limitation of path names: Sub-Class (Cause)
Improper validation of recipient address in deliver message : Sub-Class (Cause)
Injection vulnerability: Sub-Class (Cause)
Integer overflow: Sub-Class (Cause)
Integer underflow: Sub-Class (Cause)
Missed validation of pointers: Sub-Class (Cause)
Stack-based buffer overflow: Sub-Class (Cause)
Unspecified vulnerability: Sub-Class (Cause)
Use-after-free vulnerability: Sub-Class (Cause)

CVE: Class
CVE-2012-0507: Sub-Class (CVE)
CVE-2017-0199: Sub-Class (CVE)

Effect: Class
Heap-based buffer overflow trigger: Sub-Class (Effect)
Improper handling of the opaqueBackground property: Sub-Class (Effect)
Incorrect access: Sub-Class (Effect)
System state corruption: Sub-Class (Effect)
ValueOf function override: Sub-Class (Effect)

Impact: Class
Affect availability: Sub-Class (Impact)

Affect confidentiality: Sub-Class (Impact)
Affect integrity: Sub-Class (Impact)
Arbitrary JavaScript code execution: Sub-Class (Impact)
Arbitrary file access: Sub-Class (Impact)
Arbitrary files upload: Sub-Class (Impact)
Arbitrary files writing: Sub-Class (Impact)
Authentication process finalization: Sub-Class (Impact)
Code execution: Sub-Class (Impact)
Denial of service: Sub-Class (Impact)
Download system files download: Sub-Class (Impact)
Elevation of Privilege: Sub-Class: (Impact)
Information Disclosure: Sub-Class (Impact)
Information leak: Sub-Class (Impact)
Internal API functions access: Sub-Class (Impact)
Intranet IP addresses existence determination: Sub-Class (Impact)
Intranet hostnames existence determination: Sub-Class (Impact)
Local pathnames existence determination: Sub-Class (Impact)
Privileged commands execution: Sub-Class (Impact)
Privileges access: Sub-Class (Impact)
Read-only access to unauthorized resources: Sub-Class (Impact)
Security Feature Bypass: Sub-Class (Impact)
Sensitive information access: Sub-Class (Impact)
UNC share pathnames existence determination: Sub-Class (Impact)
Unauthorized access: Sub-Class (Impact)
Unspecified impact: Sub-Class (Impact)
Cross-site scripting (XSS) attacks: Sub-Class (Impact)

Ransomware: Class
AKBUILDER: Sub-Class (Ransomware)
IRAN LEAK: Sub-Class (Ransomware)
PETYA: Sub-Class (Ransomware)
RUSSIA LEAK: Sub-Class (Ransomware)
WANNACRY: Sub-Class (Ransomware)

Technique: Class
Direct Volume Access: Sub-Class (Technique) Exploit Public-Facing Application: Sub-Class (Technique)
Exploitation of Remote Services: Sub-Class (Technique)
Exploitation for Client Execution: Sub-Class (Technique)
Exploitation for Privilege Escalation : Sub-Class (Technique)
File and Directory Discovery: Sub-Class (Technique)
Input Injection: Sub-Class (Technique)

Tactic: Class
Defense Evasion: Sub-Class (Tactic)
Discovery: Sub-Class (Tactic)
Execution: Sub-Class (Tactic)
Initial Access: Sub-Class (Tactic)
Lateral Movement: Sub-Class (Tactic)

ObjectProperty

AssociatedToTactic: : ObjectProperty
CausedBy: ObjectProperty
ExploitedBy: ObjectProperty
ExploitedThrough: ObjectProperty
Exploits: ObjectProperty
HasImpact: ObjectProperty
LeadsTo: ObjectProperty &
OriginatedBy: ObjectProperty
PerformedThrough: ObjectProperty
RelatedToCause: ObjectProperty
UsesTechnique: : ObjectProperty

    DataProperty
Local: DataProperty
Remote: DataProperty
Unauthorized: DataProperty

FIGURE 4.15
Class hierarchy depicting the impacts connected to Ransomware and CVE sub-classes

As shown in Figure 4.15 the class hierarchy, in the tree-structure disposition of classes, presents the correspondences of the *Ransomware* with the *Impact* and *CVE* as well as a more extensive view including the *Effect* in Figure 4.16. The description of the relational framework in OWL language is more expressively provided as depicted in Figure 4.17 and Figure 4.18. The ontology configuration development is strictly supported by the usage of the graph generated by the implementation of the model training which gathers the information partitioned in the main classes with all the corresponding values detected in the pattern approach and in the automatizing step.

4.2.2   Integration of ATT&CK

The ontology framework has been organized, as broadly described in the previous sections, in a hierarchical structure where the main classes are represented by the semantic chain retrieved in the CVE prose descriptions and then by the *CVE*, *Ransomware* and also the *Tactic* and *Technique*. These last two classes have been included to enable a knowledge systematization related to ransomware complete and fully compliant with the attack behavior approach analysis. Per each vulnerability a Ransomware uses a specific Technique, which in turn is connected with a specific Tactic according to the taxonomy provided by Mitre. In

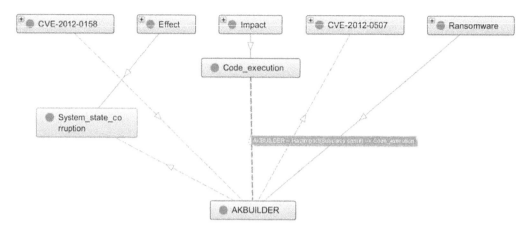

FIGURE 4.16
Effects related to AKBUILDER ransomware.

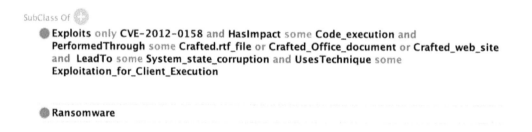

FIGURE 4.17
Relational framework constructed for AKBUILDER Ransomware.

FIGURE 4.18
Relational framework constructed for IRAN LEAK Ransomware.

this sense, the population of this information in the ontology started with the analysis of the relations detected by the experts of the domain within the source corpus. What follows is a synthetic overview of a few ransomware exploiting a pair of CVE with a determined technique:

- AKBUILDER exploits:
  - CVE-2012-0158, using Technique T1203 (Exploitation for Client Execution) associated with Tactic *Execution*
  - CVE-2015-1641,using Technique T1203 (Exploitation for Client Execution) associated with Tactic *Execution*

- ALPHV exploits:
  - CVE-2019-7481, using Technique T1083 (File and Directory Discovery) associated with Tactic *Discovery*
  - CVE-2021-26855, using Technique T1569 (System Services)associated with Tactic *Execution*

- BLACK KINGDOM exploits:
  - CVE-2019-11510, using Technique T1210 (Exploitation of Remote Services) associated with Tactic *Lateral Movement*
  - CVE-2019-11539, using Sub-Technique T1548.002 (Abuse Elevation Control Mechanism: Bypass User Account Control) of Technique T1548 (Abuse Elevation Control Mechanism) associated with Tactics *Privilege Escalation* and *Defense Evasion*

- BLACKCAT exploits:
  - CVE-2019-7481, using Technique T1083 (File and Directory Discovery) associated with Tactic *Discovery*
  - CVE-2021-31207, using Technique T1203 (Exploitation for Client Execution) associated with Tactic *Execution*

- CERBER exploits:
  - CVE-2010-0188, T1059 (Command and Scripting Interpreter) associated with Tactic *Execution*
  - CVE-2012-1723, T1203 (Exploitation for Client Execution) associated with Tactic *Execution*

- CHINA LEAK exploits:
  - CVE-2015-4852, using Technique T1202 (Indirect Command Execution)associated with Tactic *Defense Evasion*
  - CVE-2017-6327, using Technique T1068 (Exploitation for Privilege Escalation) associated with Tactic *Privilege Escalation*

- CK exploits:
  - CVE-2021-34473, using Technique T1190 (Exploit Public-Facing Application) associated with Tactic *Initial Access*
  - CVE-2021-34523, using Technique T1068 (Exploitation for Privilege Escalation) associated with Tactic *Privilege Escalation*

- CRYPTOASYOU exploits:
  - CVE-2010-0188, using Technique T1059 (Command and Scripting Interpreter) associated with Tactic *Execution*
  - CVE-2015-0311, using Technique T1203 (Exploitation for Client Execution) associated with Tactic *Execution*

- CRYPTOFORTRESS exploits:
  - CVE-2013-2551, using Technique T1203 (Exploitation for Client Execution) associated with Tactic *Execution*

  – CVE-2013-7331, using Technique T1016 (System Network Configuration Discovery) associated with Tactic *Discovery*

- IRAN LEAK exploits:
  – CVE-2017-0199, using Technique T1203 (Exploitation for Client Execution) associated with Tactic *Execution*
  – CVE-2021-45105, using Technique T1498 (Network Denial of Service) associated with Tactic *Impact*

- LAPSUS$ exploits:
  – CVE-2019-5591, using Technique T1592 (Gather Victim Host Information) associated with Tactic *Reconnaissance*
  – CVE-2021-44864, using Technique T1498 (Network Denial of Service) associated with Tactic *Impact*

- NORTH KOREA LEAK exploits:
  – CVE-2017-0199, using Technique T1203 (Exploitation for Client Execution) associated with Tactic *Execution*
  – CVE-2021-21551, using Sub-technique T1548.002 Abuse Elevation Control Mechanism: Bypass User Account Control) of Technique T1548 (Abuse Elevation Control Mechanism) associated with Tactics *Privilege Escalation* and *Defense Evasion*

- PETYA exploits:
  – CVE-2015-2444, using Technique T1203 (Exploitation for Client Execution) associated with Tactic *Execution*
  – CVE-2017-0144, using Technique T1190 (Exploit Public-Facing Application) associated with Tactic *Initial Access*

- RUSSIA LEAK exploits:
  – CVE-2019-11510, using Technique T1210 (Exploitation of Remote Services) associated with Tactic *Lateral Movement*
  – CVE-2021-21972, using Technique T1068 (Exploitation for Privilege Escalation)

- SODINOKIBI exploits:
  – CVE-2019-11539, using Sub-technique T1548.002 Abuse Elevation Control Mechanism: Bypass User Account Control) of Technique T1548 (Abuse Elevation Control Mechanism)
  – CVE-2019-2729, using Technique T1068 (Exploitation for Privilege Escalation)

- TESLACRYPT exploits:
  – CVE-2013-7331, using Technique T1016 (System Network Configuration Discovery) associated with Tactic *Discovery*
  – CVE-2015-0311, using Technique T1203 (Exploitation for Client Execution) associated with Tactic *Execution*

- VICE SOCIETY exploits:
  – CVE-2021-1675, using Technique T1068 (Exploitation for Privilege Escalation)

SubClass Of

  ● **Exploits** only **CVE-2019-7481** and **HasImpact** some **Read-only_access_to_unauthorized_resources** and **UsesTechnique** some **File_and_Directory_Discovery**

  ● **Ransomware**

FIGURE 4.19
ALPHV relational structure in the ontology

  – CVE-2021-34527, using Sub-technique T1547.012 (Boot or Logon Autostart Execution: Print Processors) of Technique T1547 (Boot or Logon Autostart Execution) associated with Tactics *Persistence* and *Privilege Escalation*

- WANNACRY exploits:
  – CVE-2017-0144, using Technique T1190 (Exploit Public-Facing Application) associated with Tactic *Initial Access*
  – CVE-2017-0147, using Technique T1592 (Gather Victim Host Information) associated with Tactic *Reconnaissance*

Given these correspondences already defined and shared by the official organism MITRE, the data within the ontology have been matched through a manual approach, with the perspective of enhancing the task by importing the D3FEND ontology described in Chapter 2. The mapping with the structural informative association Ransomware – CVE – Technique – Tactic has been formalized in the OWL language together with the classes constituting the taxonomic configuration. For instance, taking the first two examples of AKBUILDER and ALPHV, the source corpus analysis provides the following relational structure:

AKBUILDER (Sub-class of *Ransomware*) **Exploits** only CVE-2012-0158 and **HasImpact** some Code execution and **PerformedThrough** Crafted.rtf file or Crafted Office document or Crafted web site and **LeadTo** some System state corruption and **UsesTechnique** some Exploitation for Client Execution

APLHV (Sub-class of *Ransomware*) **Exploits** only CVE-2019-7481 and **HasImpact** some Read-only access to unauthorized resources and **UsesTechnique** some File and Directory Discovery (see Figure 4.19)

4.3 Analysis and Classification Results

In this section, we provide a detailed statistical analysis of the set of CVEs and ATT&CK techniques and tactics used by ransomware available in our classification scheme as well as a semantic analysis of the main co-occurrences in the patterns retrieved in order to create a precise and functional ontology framework.

4.3.1 Statistical analysis

CVE analysis
We firstly analyzed the distribution of the severity of the exploited vulnerabilities by ransomware regarding their Common Vulnerability Scoring System (CVSS) score. The objective of this analysis is to study the scoring levels of these vulnerabilities to better understand

whether ransomware is only relying on high-score CVSS vulnerabilities. Figure 4.20 depicts for each CVSS score range the percentage of vulnerabilities used by ransomware. We mainly have observed that about 45% of vulnerabilities have a CVSS score greater than or equal to 9 with half of them with a score equal to 10. About 28% of vulnerabilities have a score less than 7. These low-score vulnerabilities are usually not fixed or have low fix priority. Hence, our analysis confirms that CVSS score is an inefficient prioritization approach for fixing vulnerabilities since ransomware may exploit those with low scores.

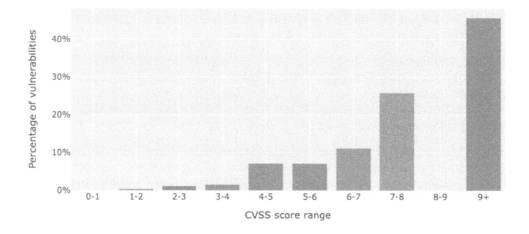

FIGURE 4.20
Distribution of ransomware exploited vulnerabilities by CVSS score range.

Secondly, we have analyzed the distribution of the number of vulnerabilities exploited by each ransomware. As depicted in Figure 4.21, we have observed that about 30% of ransomware uses a single vulnerability. The majority of ransomware, nearly 79% of them, are exploiting less than 10 vulnerabilities. Only a single ransomware, i.e., *CK*, is exploiting a high number of vulnerabilities equal to 79. The reason is that *CK* is an exploit kit used by multiple ransomware. Other ransomware, such as, *CRY, CHINA LEAK, TESLACRYPT, RUSSIA LEAK* are also exploiting a high number of vulnerabilities: 60, 49, and 32 respectively.

We subsequently analysed the number of ransomware exploiting each vulnerability (CVE) to identify the most exploited vulnerabilities. Figure 4.22 shows the distribution of CVEs by the number of their respective ransomware. We have observed that the most exploited vulnerabilities are *CVE-2015-7645* and *CVE-2015-5119* associated with 15 ransomware. These two vulnerabilities affect Adobe Flash Player and allow attackers to remotely execute arbitrary code.

The count of the vulnerabilities by their respective number of ransomware exploiting them is depicted in Figure 4.23. We have observed that around 120 vulnerabilities, which represents about 50% of the total number of vulnerabilities, are exploited, each of them by a single ransomware. Only the aforementioned 2 vulnerabilities are exploited by a high number of ransomware, 15. We have found that the majority of ransomware are using their own specific vulnerabilities and few vulnerabilities are exploited by many ransomware.

Figure 4.24 depicts the sharing ratio of vulnerabilities by their respective number of ransomware. This ratio is computed using the count of vulnerabilities shared between the ransomware. For instance, the *CK* ransomware is sharing 77 vulnerabilities with the others. We have observed that 14 ransomware have a sharing ratio of 0, i.e., they do not share vulnerabilities with any of the others. 31 ransomware are sharing a single vulnerability with the others.

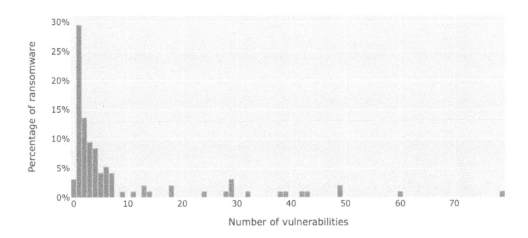

FIGURE 4.21
Distribution of the number of vulnerabilities exploited by ransomware.

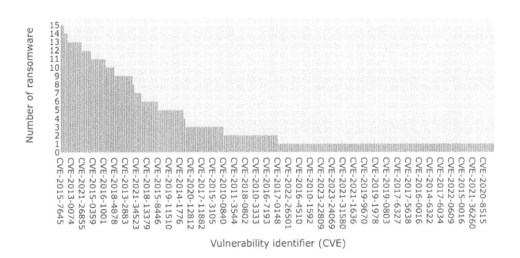

FIGURE 4.22
Distribution of CVEs by the number of ransomware exploiting each of them.

ATT&CK analysis

The analysis of tactics and techniques used by ransomware according to standard ATT&CK. relies on a dataset that we constructed and it contains a mapping between each ransomware its associated used tactic and technique. The dataset contains 174 ransomware that were active between 2007 and 2023. We mainly analysed the techniques and tactics usage over time, their common and single usage by ransomware.

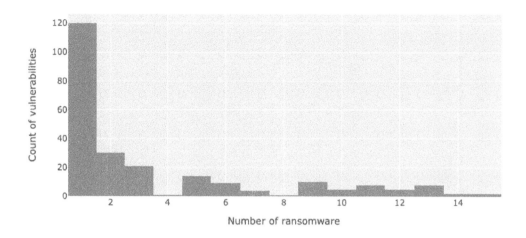

FIGURE 4.23
Count of vulnerabilities by their respective number of ransomware.

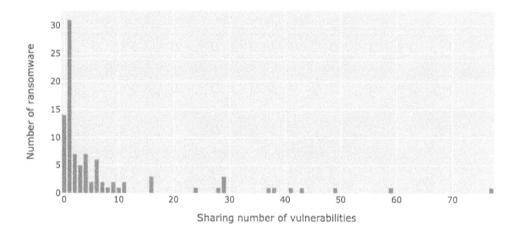

FIGURE 4.24
Sharing ratio of ransomware vulnerabilities.

Tactics analysis

We analysed the set of tactics used by each ransomware from our dataset as depicted in Figure 4.25. Each part of the figure contains 87 ransomware. We observe that the majority of ransomware is using the *execution* tactic. The first part of the figure shows more complex and sophisticated ransomware using a large number of tactics in their attack operations. In this set, we find Ryuk, China Leak, Iran Leak, Russia Leak, LockBit, CRY, etc. The second set contains less complex ransomware using only a single tactic, mainly execution.

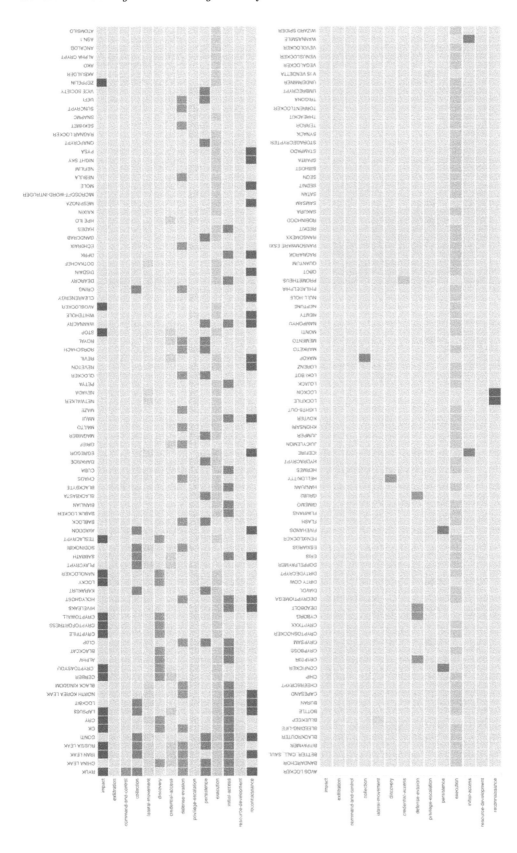

FIGURE 4.25
Tactics used by each ransomware.

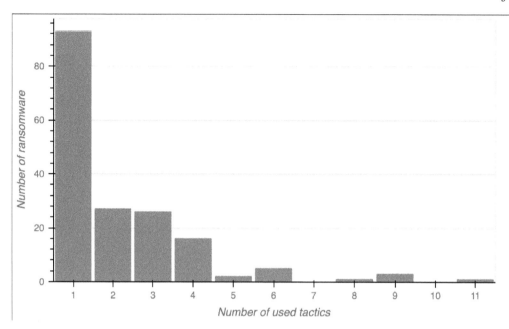

FIGURE 4.26
Distribution of Number of Ransomware by Number of Tactics Used.

Figure 4.26 shows the distribution of the number of ransomware by number of tactics used. We have observed that 50% (93) of ransomware are using a single tactic with 73 of them are using a single execution tactic. Only one ransomware which is Ryuk is exploiting 11 tactics. We have also noted that 40% of ransomware are exploiting between 2 to 4 tactics. Globally, the number of ransomware decreases when the number of used tactics increases. This result confirms that only a small number of ransomware are sophisticated or acting as a RaaS while using many tactics.

The number of used tactics and ransomware broken down by tactic is depicted in Figure 4.27. 73 ransomware among 93 instances with single tactic is mainly using the *execution* tactic. Globally, we have observed that the *execution* and *privilege-escalation* tactics are dominating and widely used by ransomware in their sets of attack tactics. These tactics are mainly fundamental to ransomware operations. However, as depicted in Figure 4.28 there are 40 ransomware (8%) that are not using the *execution* tactic in their operations.

The number of ransomware per tactic is depicted in Figure 4.28. The *execution* tactic is widely used by the majority of ransomware (77%). The second dominating tactic is the *privilege-escalation* with 35% of ransomware using this technique. The co-occurrence of the tactics and their respective number of ransomware to show how frequently different tactics appear together within the same ransomware is depicted in Figure 4.29. This provides insights into common combinations of tactics, and reflects common strategies or dependencies among tactics. We have examined that execution and privilege-escalation tactics are frequently occurring together by 42 ransomware since they complement each other in a common attack. The *execution* and privilege-escalation tactics are also often occurring with other tactics including initial-access, defense-evasion, discovery, impact, lateral-movement, persistence, and reconnaissance. The pair of tactics discovery and reconnaissance do not occur together since they mainly have similar goals. The *command-and-control* tactic has low co-occurrences with other tactics since it is only used by Ryuk in our dataset. Recognizing which tactics are commonly used together can help security teams in identifying

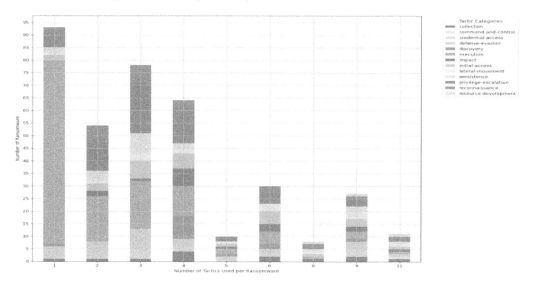

FIGURE 4.27
The number of ransomware by number of tactics and their breakdown of the specific used tactics.

potential vulnerabilities exploited in ransomware operations. Defending against one tactic might render associated tactics less effective and disrupting the attack chain.

The breakdown of tactics per ransomware and over years is depicted in Figure 4.30. We have noticed that also *execution* and *privilege-escalation* tactics are dominating over the analysis period. Since 2017, we have observed more sophistication in ransomware where they are using more tactics. However, in 2015 and in 2010, we observe also complex ransomware with many tactics. The large number of tactics used in 2015 is mainly dominated by the China LEAK ransomware and the year 2010 is dominated by the CRY rabsomware. These two major ransomware explain the large number of tactics during these two dates. The year 2021 has the largest number of used tactics, mainly because of LOCKBIT ransomware and its affiliates.

By inspecting the cumulative usage of the tactics over years as depicted in Figure 4.31, we observe the same trend dominated by two major tactics (execution and privilege-escalation). We note that in 2021, the usage of the initial-acccess tactic has a significant increase where many ransomware are exploiting public-facing applications through this tactic.

Techniques analysis

In this part, we analyze the techniques used by ransomware according to their number, names, and their distribution over years. Figure 4.32 shows the distribution of the number of used techniques according to their respective number of ransomware. We have observed that 75 (43%) ransomware are using a single technique. The breaking down of the counts of ransomware entries by the number and names of techniques they use is shown in Figure 4.33. As the execution and privilege-escalation tactics are dominating according to our first analysis, we have also remarked that the techniques associated with these tactics are dominating. Few ransomware are using a large number of techniques. These ransomware are China Leak(18 techniques), Ruyk(16 techniques), RUSSIA LEAK(13 techniques) and IRAN LEAK (11 techniques). Lockbit ransomware is using 7 techniques. These dominating execution techniques are Exploitation for Client Execution, Command and Scripting

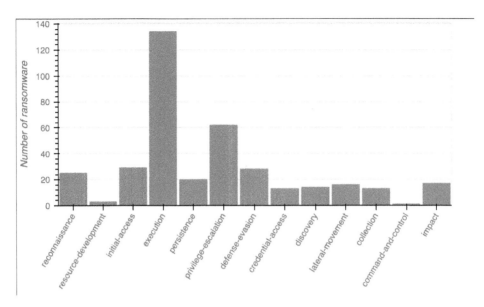

FIGURE 4.28
Number of ransomware for each used tactic.

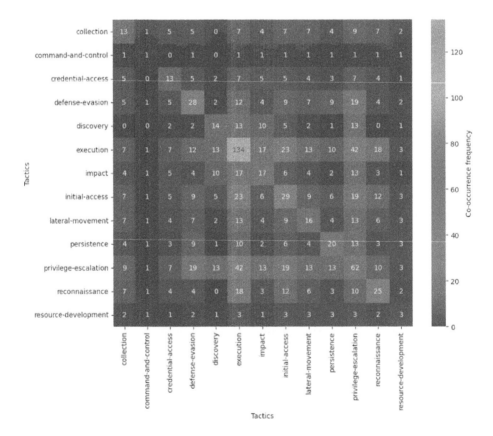

FIGURE 4.29
Co-occurrence matrix of tactics.

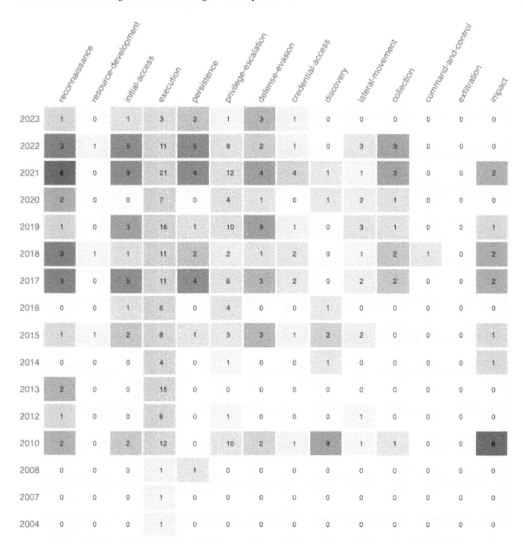

FIGURE 4.30
Used tactics over years and by the number of ransomware.

interpreter. For privilege escalation, we mainly find the Exploitation of Privilege Escalation technique.

We have analysed the sharing number of techniques between ransomware as depicted in Figure 4.34. Few ransomware, only 2, have a sharing number of techniques equal to 0. These ransomware are DEADBOLT, and ROYAL that are using Modify System Image and Modify Authentication Process, respectively. A large number of ransomware 75(43%) are sharing only one technique with other ransomware.

The distribution of techniques usage over years is shown in Figure 4.35. The technique Exploitation for Client Execution is widely used over years. At a lower frequency, the Exploitation for Privilege Escalation is also used by ransomware over the period of analysis. We have observed that the technique Command and Scripting Interpreter is widely used between 2010 and 2019 for the execution tactic. In 2021, the technique Exploit Public-Facing Application has a large usage compared to other periods.

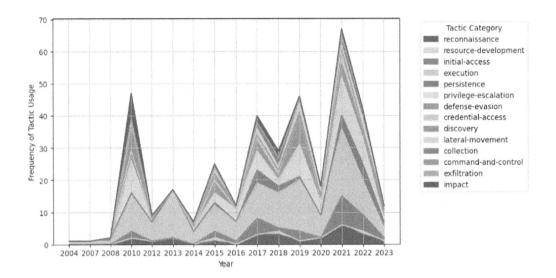

FIGURE 4.31
Cumulative usage of tactics over years.

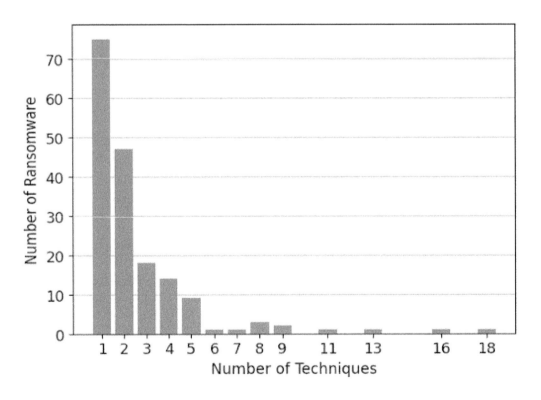

FIGURE 4.32
Number of used techniques and their respective number of ransomware.

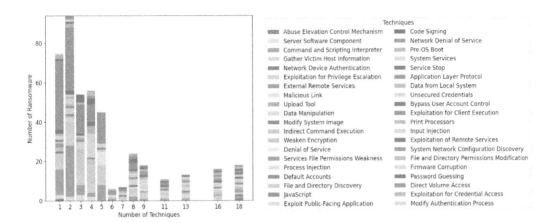

FIGURE 4.33

The used techniques per ransomware according to their count and the number of techniques.

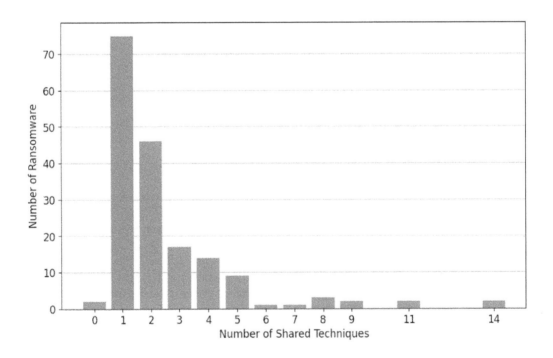

FIGURE 4.34

Sharing number of techniques between ransomware

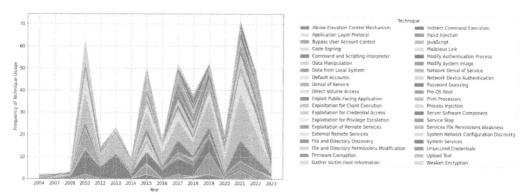

FIGURE 4.35
Distribution of techniques usage by ransomware over years.

FIGURE 4.36
Co-occurrence matrix of extracted cause and impact features.

4.3.2   Semantic analysis

The information extracted by means of the semantic annotation procedure has provided results in terms of co-occurrence levels related to the retrieved causes, impacts, actions and effects between certain vulnerabilities and ransomware. A co-occurrence matrix, depicted in Figure 4.36, supports the visualization of the combination of data studying the highest scores of impacts referred to determined causes. In this sense, it is notable that the highest value is scored for the cause *double free vulnerability* which mostly provokes the *execute code* impact, then transformed in the normalization phase in *code execution*, a data that can be observed for the cyber intelligence tasks when taking into consideration suitable measures to fight against a known set of impacts due to specific causes. Moreover, from this synthetic co-occurrence matrix a high value for the cause *unspecified vulnerability* linked to the *affect confidentiality* impact has been observed, indicating how the knowledge about the causes is weak in certain cases and the impacts are still occurring while lacking the information on the causes originating them. shows a partial view of this matrix with the highest co-occurrence values.

The semantic relations established for the classes and sub-classes represented in the ontology framework have been studied through a semantic graph organization in Gephi [19]. This visualization and exploration tool allows to have an overall picture of the connections the classes present. In particular, the node degrees of the *cause* and *impact* labels express the highest sharing ratio between ransomware and CVE, as can be seen in Figure 4.37 and Figure 4.38. The two nodes under analysis presented a score of 16 for the *cause* and 23 for the *impact*. In order to detect the communities in the semantic graph the algorithm of Modularity class has been executed and the results presented 14 communities detected (see Figure 4.39). Table 4.3 shows the first 8 communities including the names of ransomware grouped together according to highest weighted degree score.

TABLE 4.3
Communities detected and the associated ransomware.

Community	(%)	Ransomware
1	23,48 %	CRY, REVETON, TESLACRYPT,LOCKY, CERBER...
2	16,29 %	MICROSOFT-WORD-INTRUDER, DOTKACHEF, MAZE, ANCALOG...
3	15,91 %	IRAN LEAK, LAPSUS$, NEBULA, DARKSIDE, NIGHT SKY...
4	12,88 %	CK, PETYA, WHITEHOLE BLACKBYTE, SUNCRYPT...
5	10,61 %	RUSSIA LEAK, SODINOKIBI, WANNACRY, BLACK KINGDOM, SEKHMET...
6	9,47 %	NORTH KOREA LEAK, HOLYGHOST, DOPPELPAYMER, CHEERSCRYPT, AKO...
7	4,92 %	ALPHV, CHAOS, AVOSLOCKER, ASN.1, and HELLOKITTY
8	2,27%	UEFI

In the semantic graph each ransomware detected for the annotation procedure can be observed in the connection it shares with the most common *causes*, *impacts*, *actions*, and *effects* when exploiting certain vulnerabilities (Figure 4.41). In this sense, the ontology population has been facilitated since the systematized information about each ransomware supported the inclusion of structured information in the taxonomy configuration. Figure 4.42 specifically depicts the connective structure the ransomware PETYA, belonging to the third community, owns with respect to the actions, impacts, causes, and effects. As can be observed, this ransomware is strictly connected to both *double free vulnerability* and to *unspecified vulnerability* for the causes, the major impacts are related to *affect condifentiality* and the actions employed to perform the attack are several, such as those linked to *unknown vectors*, *crafted swf file*, *using an idl fragment* or *crafted parameters in unspecified api calls*. Following the same logic of knowledge organization through co-occurrence measures in Gephi, other ransomware have been observed by taking into account the semantically annotated information of CVE prose definition. For example NEBULA (see Figure 4.40) semantic connective structure shows that the most common cause is *integer overflow*, that the major impact related to this ransomware is *gain privilege* through *unkown vectors* or *crafted swf file* or *crafted web site*. These kinds of connections outlined in the graph have been included in the ontology framework as Figure 4.43 in correspondence with the CVE exploited by the ransomware NEBULA. The ransomware RUSSIA LEAK is another representative case of analysed ransomware through the graph whose information have been investigated according to the relation each *impact*, *action* and *effect* has with certain CVE as Figures 4.44 and 4.45 depict.

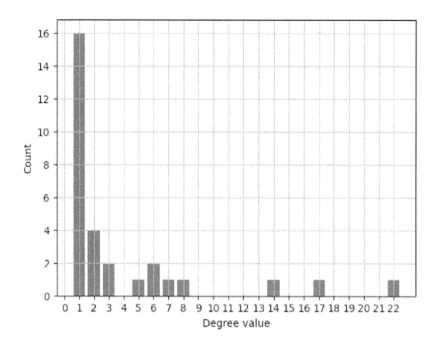

FIGURE 4.37
Distribution of the *cause* node degrees in the semantic graph.

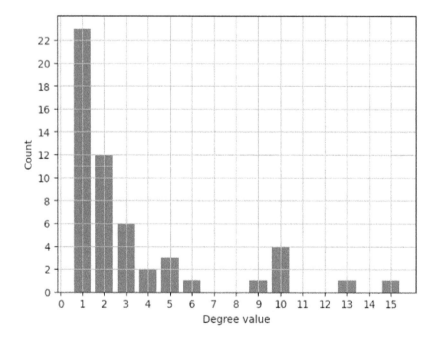

FIGURE 4.38
Distribution of the *impact* node degrees in the semantic graph.

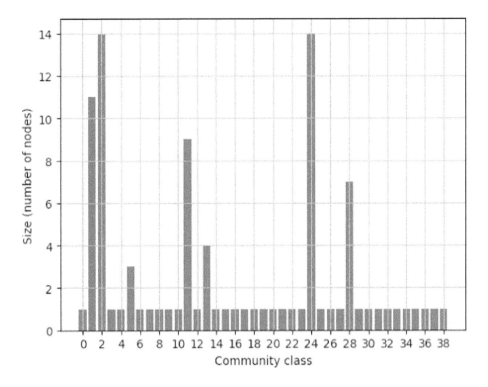

FIGURE 4.39
Ransomware communities detected.

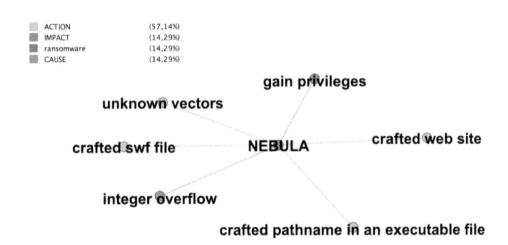

FIGURE 4.40
Connections present in the annotated texts between the NEBULA *ransomware* and the *impacts*, *causes*, and *actions*.

FIGURE 4.41

Excerpt of the connective structure of NEBULA in the ontology with one of the exploited vulnerabilities and the *impact* and *action* and *technique* associated.

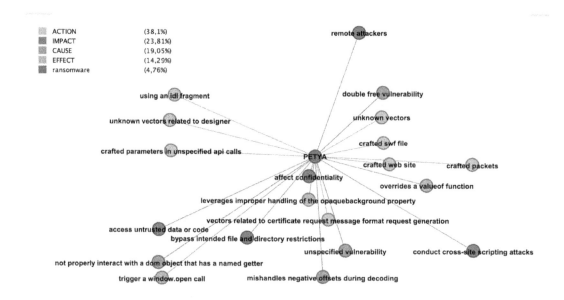

FIGURE 4.42

Connections present in the annotated texts between the PETYA *ransomware* and the *impacts*, *causes*, and *actions*.

FIGURE 4.43

Excerpt of the connective structure of PETYA in the ontology with one of the exploited vulnerabilities and the *impact* and *action* and *technique* associated.

FIGURE 4.44

Connections detected in the annotated texts between the Russia Leak *ransomware* and the *impacts*, *causes*, and *actions*.

 SubClass Of

● **Exploits** only **CVE-2019-10149** and **CausedBy** some
Improper_validation_of_recipient_address_in_deliver_message and **HasImpact** some **Code_execution** and
UsesTechnique some **Input_Injection**

● **Ransomware**

FIGURE 4.45

Excerpt of the connective structure of RUSSIALEAK in the ontology with one of the exploited vulnerabilities and the *impacts* and *actions* associated.

5

Conclusion

The research described in this book has addressed an innovative methodology in the field of cyber threat intelligence to detect and analyse the behavior of ransomware from a semantic perspective. In detail, this study has been oriented towards the construction of a classification scheme to systematize the knowledge about ransomware in order to make the connections they prove to have in given cyber episodes more explicit and possibly employed by a community of experts for defense strategies. Although, as notably remarked in the first chapters, a range of cyber threat classification systems have already been provided by the main authoritative institutions working in the Cybersecurity field of knowledge, such as CAPEC^{TM}, CVE, CPE, CWE, MAEC, Kill Chain Model, MITRE ATT&CK. The focus of these systems has been strictly referred to the attacks features configuration in a taxonomic perspective. Other works in the literature have covered the aim of developing classification tools to support the predictive systems fighting against the cyber attacks, and some of them, as Rantology or VulnOnt, specifically analysed the ransomware to create a semantic approach, specifically relating to ontologies as main systems to organize and represent domain-oriented knowledge.

The study conducted in this book has precisely considered the ransomware in relation with the vulnerabilities exploited by them to create a connective structure aimed at facilitating the description of these attacks and the typical behavior useful to predict future episodes once a new vulnerability has been discovered. To achieve this knowledge framework, the ransomware data taken into consideration to create the connective structure has been represented by the prose definitions included in the CVE published by NVD, the enumeration of vulnerabilities constantly updated with the description of the main causes originating them and the impacts generated from their exploitation, as well as the actions usually undertaken to provoke the attacks and the side effects. The semantic analysis of these CVE descriptions has shown that each of them presents a recursive textual disposition of information, and this has represented in the formalization task the path towards the creation of high-level classes when starting the configuration of the semantic tool supporting the classification of ransomware: *cause, impacts, actions, effects*. The textual descriptions contained in each CVE have been matched, through a mapping procedure in the corpus compilation phase with the source documentation about ransomware, with the instances of ransomware. The source corpus has then been compiled using by a list of CVE descriptions, each matched with the corresponding ransomware which in a given year has exploited a vulnerability, as well as ATT&CK Tactics and Technique.

By using a semantic annotation tool, Prodigy, the methodological step has initially dealt with a manual annotation of the prose descriptions to train a model able to automatically detect the salient data to include in the classification scheme. In detail, the methodology followed to build the classification tool has primarily relied on the semantic annotation of the texts within the CVE descriptions where a pattern-based approach has been defined to retrieve trigger expressions to be classified. The descriptions contained in the CVE list are characterized by a recursive way of presenting information about the vulnerabilities and this feature has represented the key starting point to structurally annotate the source

DOI: 10.1201/9781003528999-5

corpus. The model has been trained over a range of prose definitions associated with the corresponding ransomware exploiting certain vulnerabilities and has provided a supporting system from which to start populating the hierarchical configuration in the proposed ontology framework. The logic behind the ontology development has followed the principle of expanded specificity of a conceptual knowledge systematization. Hence, each class, represented by *CVE*, *Ransomware*, *Cause*, *Impact*, *Action*, *Effect*, *Tactic*, and *Technique* has been further specified in the corresponding sub-classes identified as the trigger normalized expressions detected during the semantic annotation phase. In this way, the classification system has been realized by means of OWL language. It has been extended with the inclusion of semantic relations between classes and sub-classes, properly named *Object Properties*, in order to keep the same level of granularity as the information annotated in the prose descriptions within CVE.

In the last part of the book a presentation of the main results in applying this methodological approach has been provided, specifically relating to the transformation of the trigger expressions in the texts of the CVE descriptions into the ontological configuration. One of the advantages envisaged by using ontologies as the semantic tools to represent specialized-domain knowledge lies in the fact that they are written in a language compliant with machine-readable systems. In this sense, the construction of a ransomware knowledge framework can be efficiently shared by informative systems to perform defense strategy operations as well as predictive tasks when a new vulnerability is discovered presenting similar features as the descriptions already annotated and associated with known ransomware.

Future editions could explore how advanced machine learning algorithms and artificial intelligence can be leveraged to automate and refine the process of semantic annotation and classification of ransomware-related cyber threat intelligence documents. Future iterations of the work could detail the development and implementation of real-time threat intelligence platforms that use the principles outlined in the book. Such platforms could dynamically update and refine ransomware threat models as new data becomes available, providing organizations with near-instantaneous defensive responses. Developing industry-specific threat intelligence models based on the general principles outlined in the book could be also a significant advancement. Different sectors, such as finance, healthcare, and government, face unique threats and would benefit from tailored approaches to ransomware defense.

Bibliography

[1] EAGLES (1996e). *Preliminary recommendations on corpus typology.* Consiglio Nazionale delle Ricerche. Istituto di Linguistica Computazionale, Pisa.

[2] A. Auger and C. Barrière. Pattern-based approaches to semantic relation extraction: A state-of-the-art. *Terminology*, 14:1–19, 06 2008.

[3] A. Caruso, A. Folino, F. Parisi, and R. Trunfio. A statistical method for minimum corpus size determination. In *12es Journées internationales d'Analyse statistique des Données Textuelles (JADT2014)*, Paris, France, 2014.

[4] A. Condamines. Taking genre into account when analyzing conceptual relation patterns. *Corpora*, 8:115–140, 2008.

[5] A. Abbasi and Chen. H. Applying authorship analysis to extremist-group web forum messages. *IEEE Intelligent Systems*, 20(5):67–75, 2005.

[6] Mohamad Syahir Abdullah, Anazida Binti Zainal, Mohd Aizaini Maarof, and Mohamad Nizam Kassim. Using text annotation tool on cyber security news – a review. *2019 International Conference on Cybersecurity (ICoCSec)*, pages 32–36, Negeri Sembilan, Malaysia, 2019.

[7] Stergos Afantenos and Nicolas Hernandez. What's in a message? In Afra Alishahi, Thierry Poibeau, and Aline Villavicencio, editors, *Proceedings of the EACL 2009 Workshop on Cognitive Aspects of Computational Language Acquisition*, pages 18–25, Athens, Greece, March 2009. Association for Computational Linguistics.

[8] Wadha Abdullah Al-Khater, Somaya Al-Maadeed, Abdulghani Ali Ahmed, Ali Safaa Sadiq, and Muhammad Khurram Khan. Comprehensive review of cybercrime detection techniques. *IEEE Access*, 8:137293–137311, 2020.

[9] Kadhim B Swadi AlJanabi and K Haydar. Crime data analysis using data mining techniques to improve crimes prevention procedures. In *ICIT*, 2010.

[10] Dean Allemang and Jim Hendler. Chapter 12 – counting and sets in owl. In Dean Allemang and Jim Hendler, editors, *Semantic Web for the Working Ontologist* (Second Edition), pages 249–278. Morgan Kaufmann, Boston, 2011.

[11] Grigoris Antoniou and Frank Harmelen. Web ontology language: Owl. In Steffen Staab, Rudi Studer, editors, *Handbook on Ontologies*, 2003. Institute AIFB, University of Karlsruhe, Karlsruhe, Germany.

[12] Pilar León Araúz, Arianne Reimerink, and Pamela Faber. Knowledge extraction on multidimensional concepts: Corpus pattern analysis (CPA) and concordances. In Marie-Claude L'Homme and Sylvie Szulman, editors, *Proceedings of the 8th International Conference on Terminology and Artificial Intelligence*, Toulouse, France, *November 18-20, 2009*, volume 578 of *CEUR Workshop Proceedings*. CEUR-WS.org, 2009.

[13] Nurfadilah Ariffin, Anazida Zainal, Mohd Aizaini Maarof, and Mohamad Nizam Kassim. A conceptual scheme for ransomware background knowledge construction. In *2018 Cyber Resilience Conference (CRC)*, Putrajaya, Malaysia, pages 1–4, 13–15 November 2018.

[14] Ishaan Arora, Julia Guo, Sarah Ita Levitan, Susan McGregor, and Julia Hirschberg. A novel methodology for developing automatic harassment classifiers for Twitter. In Seyi Akiwowo, Bertie Vidgen, Vinodkumar Prabhakaran, and Zeerak Waseem, editors, *Proceedings of the Fourth Workshop on Online Abuse and Harms*, pages 7–15, Online, November 2020. Association for Computational Linguistics.

[15] Adi Aviad, Krzysztof Węcel, and Witold Abramowicz. The semantic approach to cyber security. Towards ontology based body of knowledge. In Proceedings of the 14th European Conference on Cyber Warfare and Security (ECCWS - 2015), edited by Nasser Abouzakhar, 328–336. Academic Conferences and Publishing International Ltd, 2015.

[16] B. Gray. Exploring methods for evaluating corpus representativeness. 2017.

[17] Franz Baader. Description logics. pages 1–39, 09 2009.

[18] Ken Barker, Parul Awasthy, Jian Ni, and Radu Florian. IBM MNLP IE at CASE 2021 task 2: NLI reranking for zero-shot text classification. In Ali Hürriyetoğlu, editor, *Proceedings of the 4th Workshop on Challenges and Applications of Automated Extraction of Socio-political Events from Text (CASE 2021)*, pages 193–202, Online, August 2021. Association for Computational Linguistics.

[19] Mathieu Bastian, Sebastien Heymann, and Mathieu Jacomy. Gephi: An open source software for exploring and manipulating networks. 2009.

[20] Sengottuvelan P. Begam, M. R. Crime case reasoning based knowledge discovery using sentence case relative clustering for crime analyses. *International Journal of Engineering & Technology*, volume 7, pages 91–97, 2018.

[21] Madan Bhasin. Mitigating cyber threats to banking industry. *The Chartered Accountant*, pages 1619–1624, 04 2007.

[22] Maria Teresa Biagetti. Le ontologie come strumenti per l'organizzazione della conoscenza in rete, 2010, pp. 9-32. *AIDA Informazioni*, 1/2:5–32, 2010.

[23] Carlo Bianchini. S. r. ranganathan e la nascita della colon classification. *Bibliotheca*, 1:64–77, 2006.

[24] Carlo Bianchini. *Teoria e tecniche della catalogazione e delle classificazioni*. 11. 2018.

[25] Federico Bonetti, Elisa Leonardelli, Daniela Trotta, Raffaele Guarasci, and Sara Tonelli. Work hard, play hard: Collecting acceptability annotations through a 3d game. page 1740–1750, 2022.

[26] W.N. Borst. *Construction of Engineering Ontologies for Knowledge Sharing and Reuse*. Phd thesis – research ut, graduation ut, University of Twente, Netherlands, September 1997.

[27] Robert A. Bridges, Corinne L. Jones, Michael D. Iannacone, and John R. Goodall. Automatic labeling for entity extraction in cyber security. *ArXiv*, abs/1308.4941, 2013.

[28] Qusay Bsoul, Juhana Salim, and Lailatul Qadri Zakaria. An intelligent document clustering approach to detect crime patterns. *Procedia Technology*, 11:1181–1187, 2013. 4th International Conference on Electrical Engineering and Informatics, ICEEI 2013.

[29] Andrew Caines, Sergio Pastrana, Alice Hutchings, and Paula Buttery. Aggressive language in an online hacking forum. In Darja Fišer, Ruihong Huang, Vinodkumar Prabhakaran, Rob Voigt, Zeerak Waseem, and Jacqueline Wernimont, editors, *Proceedings of the 2nd Workshop on Abusive Language Online (ALW2)*, pages 66–74, Brussels, Belgium, October 2018. Association for Computational Linguistics.

[30] Araceli Alonso Campos and Irene Renau Araque. Corpus pattern analysis in determining specialised uses of verbal lexical units. *Terminalia*, pages 26–33, 2013.

[31] Enzo Cesanelli. Classificare il dominio della comunicazione secondo la teoria dei livelli di integrazione. *E-LIS*, 2008.

[32] B. Chandrasekaran, John Josephson, and V. Richard Benjamins. What are ontologies, and why do we need them? *Intelligent Systems and their Applications, IEEE*, 14:20–26, 02 1999.

[33] Kandan Chitra and Balakrishnan Subashini. Data mining techniques and its applications in banking sector. *International Journal of Emerging Technology and Advanced Engineering*, 3(8):219–226, 2013.

[34] Leshem Choshen, Dan Eldad, Daniel Hershcovich, Elior Sulem, and Omri Abend. The language of legal and illegal activity on the Darknet. In Anna Korhonen, David Traum, and Lluís Màrquez, editors, *Proceedings of the 57th Annual Meeting of the Association for Computational Linguistics*, pages 4271–4279, Florence, Italy, July 2019. Association for Computational Linguistics.

[35] Isobelle Clarke and Jack Grieve. Dimensions of abusive language on Twitter. In Zeerak Waseem, Wendy Hui Kyong Chung, Dirk Hovy, and Joel Tetreault, editors, *Proceedings of the First Workshop on Abusive Language Online*, pages 1–10, Vancouver, BC, Canada, August 2017. Association for Computational Linguistics.

[36] Lanza Claudia. *Semantic Control for the Cybersecurity Domain Investigation on the Representativeness of a Domain-Specific Terminology Referring to Lexical Variation*. CRC Press, Abingdon, Oxon, 2022.

[37] Anne Condamines. Corpus analysis and conceptual relation patterns. *Terminology*, 8:141–162, 07 2002.

[38] D. Biber Representativeness in Corpus Design. *In Literary and Linguistic Computing*, 8(4):243–257, 01 1993.

[39] Deborah Grbac Mario Corveddu Carol Rolla Di Nunzio, Alessandra. Terminologia e tassonomia: un'esperienza in biblioteca. XXIII, no. 1:193–223, 2014.

[40] Yuxin Ding, Rui Wu, and Xiao Zhang. Ontology-based knowledge representation for malware individuals and families. *Comput. Secur.*, 87(C), Nov 2019.

[41] Zhaoyun Ding, Deqi Cao, Lina Liu, Donghua Yu, Haoyang Ma, and Fei Wang. A method for discovering hidden patterns of cybersecurity knowledge based on hierarchical clustering. In *2021 IEEE Sixth International Conference on Data Science in Cyberspace (DSC)*, pages 334–338, 2021.

[42] Elena Doynikova, Andrey Fedorchenko, and Igor Kotenko. Ontology of metrics for cyber security assessment. pages 1–8, 08 2019.

[43] Suchi Dubey and Waleed Almonayirie. Uae banks financial merit diagnosis using dual-classification scheme. 12 2014.

[44] Ismail El Maarouf. Methodological aspects of corpus pattern analysis. *ICAME*, 37:119–148, 01 2013.

[45] Ana Carolina Ferreira, Benildes Coura Moreira dos Santos Maculan, and Madalena Martins Lopes Naves. Ranganathan and the faceted classification theory. 12 2017.

[46] Antonietta Folino. Tassonomie e thesauri. In *Documenti digitali*, pages 387–444. ITER srl., a cura di Roberto Guarasci, 2013.

[47] Erika De Francesco, Salvatore Iiritano, Antonino Spagnolo, and Marco Iannelli. A methodology for semi-automatic classification schema building, 2009.

[48] Beatriz Franco Martins Souza, Lenin Gil, José Reyes Román, Ignacio Panach, Oscar Pastor, Moshe Hadad, and Benny Rochwerger. A framework for conceptual characterization of ontologies and its application in the cybersecurity domain. *Software and Systems Modeling*, 21, 07 2022.

[49] Corpas Pastor G. and Seghiri M. Size matters: A quantitative approach to corpus representativeness. *in Language, translation, reception. To honor Julio César Santoyo, Universidad de León*, pages 1–35, 2010.

[50] G. Leech. The state of the art in corpus linguistics. *in Aijmer K. and Altenberg B. (eds.) English Corpus Linguistics: Studies in Honour of JaJan Svartvik*, London: Longman, pages 8–29., 1991.

[51] G. Zagrebelsky. *Il sistema costituzionale delle fonti del diritto*. UTET, Turin, 1984.

[52] Borgo Stefano Masolo Claudio Oltramari Alessandro Guarino Nicola Gaio, Silvia. Un'introduzione all'ontologia dolce. *AIDA Informazioni*, 1/2:107–125, 10 2010.

[53] Joaquín Gayoso-Cabada, Antonio Sarasa-Cabezuelo, and José-Luis Sierra. Document annotation tools: Annotation classification mechanisms. In *Proceedings of the Sixth International Conference on Technological Ecosystems for Enhancing Multiculturality*, TEEM'18, page 889–895, New York, NY, USA, 2018. Association for Computing Machinery.

[54] Lee Gillam, Mariam Tariq, and Khurshid Ahmad. Terminology and the construction of ontology. *Terminology. International Journal of Theoretical and Applied Issues in Specialized Communication*, 11(1):55–81, 2005.

[55] Claudio Gnoli. *Classificazione a faccette*. Associazione Italiane Biblioteche (AIB), 2004.

[56] Thomas R. Gruber. Toward principles for the design of ontologies used for knowledge sharing. 43, 5-6:1995, 2014.

[57] Raffaele Guarasci, Stefano Silvestri, Giuseppe De Pietro, Hamido Fujita, and Massimo Esposito. Bert syntactic transfer: A computational experiment on Italian, French and English languages. *Computer Speech and Language*, 71, 2022.

[58] Nicola Guarino. Understanding, building and using ontologies. *International Journal of Human-Computer Studies*, 46(2):293–310, 1997.

[59] Nicola Guarino, Daniel Oberle, and Steffen Staab. *What Is an Ontology?*, pages 1–17. 05 2009.

[60] Mauro Guerrini. Classificazioni bibliografiche. In *Documenti digitali*, pages 371–385. ITER srl., a cura di Roberto Guarasci, 2013.

[61] Ismail El Maarouf, Hanks Patrick, and Michael Oakes. Flexibility of multiword expressions and corpus pattern analysis. pages 93–119, 2017.

[62] Birger Hjørland. Concept theory. *Journal of the American Society for Information Science and Technology*, 60:1519–1536, 08 2009.

[63] Birger Hjørland. Knowledge organization (ko). *KNOWLEDGE ORGANIZATION*, 434(6):475–484, 01 2016.

[64] Susan Hunston and Hang Su. Patterns, constructions, and local grammar: A case study of 'evaluation'. *Applied Linguistics*, 40:567–593, 08 2019.

[65] I. Meyer. Extracting knowledge-rich contexts for terminography: A conceptual and methodological framework. In *Recent Advances in Computational Terminology*, pages 279–302. John Benjamins, Amsterdam, 2001.

[66] Pearson J. *Terms in Context*. John Benjamins, Amsterdam, 1998.

[67] R. Jayabrabu, V. Saravanan, and J. Jebamalar Tamilselvi. A framework for fraud detection system in automated data mining using intelligent agent for better decision making process. In *2014 International Conference on Green Computing Communication and Electrical Engineering (ICGCCEE)*, Coimbatore, India, pages 1–8, 2014.

[68] Yan Jia, Yulu Qi, Huaijun Shang, Rong Jiang, and Aiping Li. A practical approach to constructing a knowledge graph for cybersecurity. *Engineering*, 4(1):53–60, 2018.

[69] Arnav Joshi, Ravendar Lal, Tim Finin, and Anupam Joshi. Extracting cybersecurity related linked data from text. pages 252–259, 09 2013.

[70] Masoudeh Keshavarzi and Hamid Ghaffari. An ontology-driven framework for knowledge representation of digital extortion attacks. *Computers in Human Behavior*, 139:107520, 02 2023.

[71] Sanghee Kim, Rob Bracewell, Saeema Ahmed-Kristensen, and Ken Wallace. Semantic annotation to support automatic taxonomy classification. 05 2006.

[72] Atanas Kiryakov, Borislav Popov, Damyan Ognyanoff, Dimitar Manov, Angel Kirilov, and Miroslav Goranov. Semantic annotation, indexing, and retrieval. In Dieter Fensel, Katia Sycara, and John Mylopoulos, editors, *The Semantic Web – ISWC 2003*, pages 484–499, 2003. Springer Berlin Heidelberg.

[73] Jana Kurrek, Haji Mohammad Saleem, and Derek Ruths. Towards a comprehensive taxonomy and large-scale annotated corpus for online slur usage. In Seyi Akiwowo, Bertie Vidgen, Vinodkumar Prabhakaran, and Zeerak Waseem, editors, *Proceedings of the Fourth Workshop on Online Abuse and Harms*, pages 138–149, Online, November 2020. Association for Computational Linguistics.

[74] L. Lefeuvre. *Analyse des marqueurs de relations conceptuelles en corpus spécialisé : recensement, évaluation et caractérisation en fonction du domaine et du genre textuel.* PhD thesis, 2017. Thèse de doctorat dirigée par Condamines, Anne et Rebeyrolle, Josette Sciences du langage Toulouse 2 2017.

[75] Monica Lagazio, Nazneen Sherif, and Mike Cushman. A multi-level approach to understanding the impact of cyber crime on the financial sector. *Computers & Security*, 45:58–74, 2014.

[76] Maria Cristina Lavazza. La colon classification. struttura, radici filosofiche e diffusione. *AIB Web Contributi*, 2002.

[77] Geoffrey Leech. Corpora and theories of linguistics performance. In J. Svartvik (ed.), editor, *Directions in Corpus Linguistics: Proceedings of Nobel Symposium*, pages 105–122, Berlin: Mouton de Gruyter, 1992.

[78] K. Chitra Lekha and S. Prakasam. Data mining techniques in detecting and predicting cyber crimes in banking sector. In *2017 International Conference on Energy, Communication, Data Analytics and Soft Computing (ICECDS)*, Chennai, India, pages 1639–1643, 2017.

[79] Yongxin Liao, Mario Lezoche, Hervé Panetto, and Nacer Boudjlida. Semantic annotation model definition for systems interoperability. pages 61–70, 10 2011.

[80] Kai Liu, Fei Wang, Zhaoyun Ding, Sheng Liang, Zhengfei Yu, and Yun Zhou. A review of knowledge graph application scenarios in cyber security, 2022.

[81] M. A. Hearst. Automatic acquisition of hyponyms from large text corpora. In *COLING 1992 Volume 2: The 15th International Conference on Computational Linguistics*, Nantes, France, 1992.

[82] Christos Makris, Georgios Pispirigos, and Michael Angelos Simos. Text semantic annotation: A distributed methodology based on community coherence. *Algorithms*, 13(7), 2020.

[83] Sanjeev Sofat Manpreet kaur, Divya Bansal. Study of cyber frauds and bcp related attacks in financial institutes. *International Journal of Information & Computation Technology*, volume 4, pages 1647–1652, 2014.

[84] Vittorio Marino. Classificazioni per il web i vantaggi dell'adozione di schemi a faccette. *AIB-WEB. Contributi*, 2004.

[85] Alberto Marradi. Classificazioni, tipologie, tassonomie. 1992.

[86] Fiammetta Marulli, Marco Pota, Massimo Esposito, Alessandro Maisto, and Raffaele Guarasci. Tuning syntaxnet for pos tagging italian sentences. *Lecture Notes on Data Engineering and Communications Technologies*, 13:314–324, 2018.

[87] Fulvio Mazzocchi and Claudio Gnoli. Il vaisesika e le categorie di ranganathan. 3-4/2006:17–28, 01 2006.

[88] Nikki McNeil, Robert A. Bridges, Michael D. Iannacone, Bogdan D. Czejdo, Nicolas Perez, and John R. Goodall. PACE: pattern accurate computationally efficient bootstrapping for timely discovery of cyber-security concepts. *CoRR*, abs/1308.4648, 2013.

[89] Manisha More, Mrs.Meenakshi P.Jadhav, and Dr.K.M.Nalawade. Online banking and cyber attacks: The current scenario. 5:743–749, 01 2016.

[90] Sumit More, Mary Matthews, Anupam Joshi, and Tim Finin. A knowledge-based approach to intrusion detection modeling. In *2012 IEEE Symposium on Security and Privacy Workshops*, pages 75–81, 2012.

[91] Sumit More, Mary Matthews, Anupam Joshi, and Timothy W. Finin. A knowledge-based approach to intrusion detection modeling. *2012 IEEE Symposium on Security and Privacy Workshops*, pages 75–81, 2012.

[92] David A. Mundie and David M. McIntire. An ontology for malware analysis. *2013 International Conference on Availability, Reliability and Security*, pages 556–558, Regensburg, Germany, 2013.

[93] Fortunee Musabeyezu. Comparative study of annotation tools and techniques, 2019.

[94] Kanika Narang and Chris Brew. Abusive language detection using syntactic dependency graphs. In Seyi Akiwowo, Bertie Vidgen, Vinodkumar Prabhakaran, and Zeerak Waseem, editors, *Proceedings of the Fourth Workshop on Online Abuse and Harms*, pages 44–53, Online, November 2020. Association for Computational Linguistics.

[95] María Auxilio Medina Nieto. An overview of ontologies. *Universidad De Las Américas Puebla, Interactive and Cooperative Technologies Lab*, 2003.

[96] Leo Obrst, Penny Chase, and Richard Markeloff. Developing an ontology of the cyber security domain. In *Semantic Technologies for Intelligence, Defense, and Security*, 2012.

[97] Philip O'Kane, Sakir Sezer, and Domhnall Carlin. Evolution of ransomware. *IET Networks*, 7(5):321–327, 2018.

[98] Alessandro Oltramari, Lorrie Faith Cranor, Robert J. Walls, and Patrick McDaniel. Building an ontology of cyber security. *CEUR Workshop Proceedings*, 1304:54–61, 2014. 9th Conference on Semantic Technology for Intelligence, Defense, and Security, STIDS 2014 ; Conference date: 18-11-2014 Through 21-11-2014.

[99] Enghin Omer. Using machine learning to identify jihadist messages on twitter, 2015.

[100] Kadir Bulut Ozler, Kate Kenski, Steve Rains, Yotam Shmargad, Kevin Coe, and Steven Bethard. Fine-tuning for multi-domain and multi-label uncivil language detection. In Seyi Akiwowo, Bertie Vidgen, Vinodkumar Prabhakaran, and Zeerak Waseem, editors, *Proceedings of the Fourth Workshop on Online Abuse and Harms*, pages 28–33, Online, November 2020. Association for Computational Linguistics.

[101] Mary C. Parmelee. Toward an ontology architecture for cyber-security standards. In *Semantic Technologies for Intelligence, Defense, and Security*, 2010.

[102] Hanks Patrick. Corpus pattern analysis. pages 87–97, 2004.

[103] Maria Teresa Pazienza. Ontologie e web semantico : proprietà e problematiche connesse al loro uso diffuso. *AIDA Informazioni*, 1/2:33–61, 2010.

[104] Fernando Pech, Alicia Martínez-Rebollar, Hugo Estrada Esquivel, and Yasmin Hernandez. Semantic annotation of unstructured documents using concepts similarity. *Scientific Programming*, 2017:1–10, 12 2017.

[105] Peter Phandi, Amila Silva, and Wei Lu. SemEval-2018 task 8: Semantic extraction from CybersecUrity REports using natural language processing (SecureNLP). In Marianna Apidianaki, Saif M. Mohammad, Jonathan May, Ekaterina Shutova, Steven Bethard, and Marine Carpuat, editors, *Proceedings of the 12th International Workshop on Semantic Evaluation*, pages 697–706, New Orleans, Louisiana, June 2018. Association for Computational Linguistics.

[106] R. Miyata and K. Kageura. Building controlled bilingual terminologies for the municipal domain and evaluating them using a coverage estimation approach. *In Terminology. International Journal of Theoretical and Applied Issues in Specialized Communication*, 24(2):149–180, 2018.

[107] S. R. Ranganathan. *Colon classification: basic classification*. Madras Library Association Publication, 1960.

[108] S. Dutta, M. Zaki, A. Gittens, C. Aggarwal, N. Rastogi. Malont: An ontology for malware threat intelligence. *International Workshop on Deployable Machine Learning for Security Defense*, San Diego, CA, 2022.

[109] Gathika Rathnayake, Thushari Atapattu, Mahen Herath, Georgia Zhang, and Katrina Falkner. Enhancing the identification of cyberbullying through participant roles. In Seyi Akiwowo, Bertie Vidgen, Vinodkumar Prabhakaran, and Zeerak Waseem, editors, *Proceedings of the Fourth Workshop on Online Abuse and Harms*, pages 89–94, Online, November 2020. Association for Computational Linguistics.

[110] Francesco Re, Daniel Vegh, Dennis Atzenhofer, and Niklas Stoehr. Team "DaDeFrNi" at CASE 2021 task 1: Document and sentence classification for protest event detection. In Ali Hürriyetoğlu, editor, *Proceedings of the 4th Workshop on Challenges and Applications of Automated Extraction of Socio-political Events from Text (CASE 2021)*, pages 171–178, Online, August 2021. Association for Computational Linguistics.

[111] Giuseppe Rizzo and Raphaël Troncy. NERD: A framework for unifying named entity recognition and disambiguation extraction tools. In Frédérique Segond, editor, *Proceedings of the Demonstrations at the 13th Conference of the European Chapter of the Association for Computational Linguistics*, pages 73–76, Avignon, France, April 2012. Association for Computational Linguistics.

[112] Renato Rocha Souza, Douglas Tudhope, and Mauricio Almeida. Towards a taxonomy of kos: Dimensions for classifying knowledge organization systems. *KNOWLEDGE ORGANIZATION*, 39:179–192, 01 2012.

[113] Ina Roesiger, Julia Bettinger, Johannes Schäfer, Michael Dorna, and Ulrich Heid. Acquisition of semantic relations between terms: how far can we get with standard NLP tools? In Patrick Drouin, Natalia Grabar, Thierry Hamon, Kyo Kageura, and Koichi Takeuchi, editors, *Proceedings of the 5th International Workshop on Computational Terminology (Computerm2016)*, pages 41–51, Osaka, Japan, December 2016. The COLING 2016 Organizing Committee.

[114] Hunston S. Corpora in applied linguistics. *Cambridge Applied Linguistics*, Cambridge University Press, 2002.

[115] Anna Schmidt and Michael Wiegand. A survey on hate speech detection using natural language processing. In Lun-Wei Ku and Cheng-Te Li, editors, *Proceedings of the Fifth International Workshop on Natural Language Processing for Social Media*, pages 1–10, Valencia, Spain, April 2017. Association for Computational Linguistics.

[116] Alfredo Serrai. *Le Classificazioni. Idee e materiali per una teoria e per una storia.* Biblioteconomia e bibliografia. Saggi e studi, vol. 10 1977, 1977.

[117] Jiaming Shen, Yunyi Zhang, Heng Ji, and Jiawei Han. Corpus-based open-domain event type induction. In Marie-Francine Moens, Xuanjing Huang, Lucia Specia, and Scott Wen-tau Yih, editors, *Proceedings of the 2021 Conference on Empirical Methods in Natural Language Processing*, pages 5427–5440, Online and Punta Cana, Dominican Republic, November 2021. Association for Computational Linguistics.

[118] Leslie F. Sikos. Cybersecurity knowledge graphs. *Knowledge and Information Systems*, 65(9):3511–3531, 2023.

[119] John Sinclair. *Looking Up: An account of the COBUILD Project in Lexical Computing.* London and Glasgow: Collins ELT, 1987.

[120] Anoop Singhal and Duminda Wijesekera. Ontologies for modeling enterprise level security metrics. *ACM International Conference Proceeding Series*, 04 2010.

[121] Tushar Sonawane, Shirin naaz Shaikh, Rahul Shinde, Shaista Shaikh, and Asif Sayyad. Crime pattern analysis, visualization and prediction using data mining. *International Journal of Advance Research and Innovative Ideas in Education*, 1:681–686, 2015.

[122] Pontus Stenetorp, Sampo Pyysalo, Goran Topic, Tomoko Ohta, Sophia Ananiadou, and Junichi Tsujii. brat: a web-based tool for nlp-assisted text annotation. In *Conference of the European Chapter of the Association for Computational Linguistics*, Avignon, France, 2012.

[123] Wolfgang Stock. Concepts and semantic relations in information science. *JASIST*, 61:1951–1969, 10 2010.

[124] Petra Storjohann. Corpus-driven vs. corpus-based approach to the study of relational patterns. Proceedings of the Corpus Linguistics Conference 2005, Birmingham, 2016. University of Birmingham.

[125] Rudi Studer, V. Richard Benjamins, and Dieter Fensel. Knowledge engineering: Principles and methods. *Data & Knowledge Engineering*, 25(1):161–197, 1998.

[126] Takeshi Takahashi and Youki Kadobayashi. Reference ontology for cybersecurity operational information. *The Computer Journal*, 10 2014.

[127] Daniela Trotta, Raffaele Guarasci, Elisa Leonardelli, and Sara Tonelli. Monolingual and cross-lingual acceptability judgments with the Italian cola corpus. page 2929 – 2940, 2021.

[128] Michael Uschold and Michael Grüninger. Ontologies: Principles, methods and applications. *The Knowledge Engineering Review*, 11, 01 1996.

[129] Michael Uschold and Martin King. Towards a methodology for building ontologies. 1995.

[130] Sida Wang and Christopher D. Manning. Baselines and bigrams: simple, good sentiment and topic classification. In *Proceedings of the 50th Annual Meeting of the Association for Computational Linguistics: Short Papers – Volume 2*, ACL '12, page 90–94, USA, 2012. Association for Computational Linguistics.

[131] Wayne A. Wiegand. The Amherst method: The origins of the Dewey decimal classification scheme. *Libraries & Culture*, 33:175–194, 1998.

[132] Hongsheng Xu, Luosheng An, and Ganglong Fan. *Improvement of Semantic Anno- tation Method in Semantic Internet of Things Based on Conceptual Ontology Model: Applications and Techniques in Cyber Security and Intelligence*, pages 1276–1282. 01 2019.

[133] Seid Muhie Yimam, Hizkiel Mitiku Alemayehu, Abinew Ayele, and Chris Biemann. Exploring Amharic sentiment analysis from social media texts: Building annotation tools and classification models. In Donia Scott, Nuria Bel, and Chengqing Zong, edi- tors, *Proceedings of the 28th International Conference on Computational Linguistics*, pages 1048–1060, Barcelona, Spain (Online), December 2020. International Commit- tee on Computational Linguistics.

[134] Li Yuan-jie and Cao Jian. Web service classification based on automatic semantic annotation and ensemble learning. In *2012 IEEE 26th International Parallel and Distributed Processing Symposium Workshops & PhD Forum*, pages 2274–2279, 2012.

[135] Marcia Zeng. Knowledge organization systems (kos). *Knowledge Organization*, 35:160–182, 01 2008.

[136] Hanqi Zhang, Xi Xiao, Francesco Mercaldo, Shiguang Ni, Fabio Martinelli, and Arun Kumar. Classification of ransomware families with machine learning based on n -gram of opcodes. *Future Generation Computer Systems*, 90, 08 2018.

[137] Xiaojuan Zhao, Rong Jiang, Yue Han, Aiping Li, and Zhichao Peng. A survey on cybersecurity knowledge graph construction. *Computers & Security*, 136:103524, 2024.